BEST NEBRASKA TEEN WRITING

2022

BEST NEBRASKA TEEN WRITING

2022

Hastings College Press | Hastings, Nebraska

ISBN: 978-1-942885-86-3

Cover image by A. Stowe.

Contents

Short Story

Novel Writing

Poetry

Humor

Critical Essay

Personal Essay & Memoir

Journalism

Introduction

After launching the Nebraska Scholastic Writing Awards in 2019 to become the first Nebraska school in many years to be an Affiliate Partner of the Alliance for Young Artists & Writers, Hastings College is proud to honor 24 students who earned awards for the 2022 competition. We invited students age 13 and above from all 93 counties within the state of Nebraska to submit their writing in one of ten categories, such as Critical Essay, Poetry, and Short Story. Graduating seniors also had the option of submitting a Writing Portfolio, a collection of works that demonstrate the writer's technical versatility. All of this year's submissions were read by a jury of Hastings College faculty, staff, and students. The original work featured in this publication showcases the creativity of our award recipients, whom we celebrated at a virtual awards ceremony that featured YA literature author Marshall Highet as keynote speaker.

The Scholastic Art & Writing Awards program, established in 1923 by Maurice R. Robinson, the founder of Scholastic Inc., identifies teenagers with exceptional artistic and literary talent and brings their remarkable work to a national audience. All works are blindly adjudicated based on originality, technical skill, and the emergence of personal vision or voice, first on a regional level by more than 100 local affiliates of the Alliance, and then nationally by an impressive panel of industry experts. Students at the regional level are awarded an Honorable Mention, Silver Key, or Gold Key distinction. Gold Key work then advances to national adjudication to receive Gold Medals or Silver Medals. Each region also nominates works for American Voices & Visions Medals, the highest regional honor.

Annually, the Alliance partners with individuals, foundations, and corporations to offer scholarship opportunities for students in certain categories or addressing particular themes. National Medalists' works are published in national publications and on the Alliance's website, artandwriting.org. Select writing is published in *The Best Teen Writing* annual anthology. The Alliance strives to teach young students to develop a strong creative capacity along with celebrating the role of art and literature in society.

Dr. Patricia Oman
Hastings College
Hastings, NE

science fiction & fantasy

FREEDOM TASTES LIKE BLOOD

ASHLEY BINSTOCK

Grade 12. Bishop Neumann Central High School, Wahoo, NE. Marisa Grady, Educator. Gold Key. American Voices Nominee.

Portfolio Gold Key

I feel myself slipping as the primitive roof grows slick with rain. Wedging my foot between the slats, I find balance, trepidation lighting firecrackers at my fingertips. *Slow, watch your step. Not yet, but soon. Not yet but soon, not yet but*—I am a clock hand forever chasing yet unable to capture time. My thoughts are always heightened before, as if by running fast enough they might escape bodily confinement, dragging my disease along with them. That is what it is—a disease. Not to be confused with blessings, powers, or virtue of any kind. My ears roar in the kind of rain that comes in sheets, as though if you stared hard enough you could read the melting pages. Silence stirs below, yet soon the peace will be broken.

Soon, but not yet.

◇◇◇◇◇

Baba hated villains. In my earliest memories we fought with wooden swords pulled from tree branches, slashing against sinister bed sheets he strung up to hang like shadows. Together we would lurk toward the misshapen and unusually colorful monsters until, like snakes, we lunged. Baba never failed and the bed sheets never won. After much deliberation and Mummy's persuasive charms, she could eventually lure him toward our pilafs of rice that she insisted were not going to wait for victory before cooling. Settling around the mat, we dug in as the comfort of rising spices stung my nose.

The scriptures say that to find love is to find your center. Mummy saw Baba. She saw the way he delicately strung up his weapons to hang like art along our walls. How he protected me through informed talk of worldly dangers. She understood as if from the eye of the hurricane, she could feel the breadth of the storm. I wish I had felt the same, but it had not mattered. In the end, death would take her away from us, and Baba would forever lose the target of his heart.

Mostly, I don't blame Mummy for dying, but there are moments. Moments when my legs refuse the command of my heart. When, despite every nerve in my body wailing in protest, I am driven further into the wild heat of disaster. Saving everyone else, I die day by day in the cold agony of knowing, *feeling* the depth of pain he'll allow me to endure. I hate her for not seeing what Baba would do to me. It is only for a fraction of time when I am tired of hating myself. Yet I am glad she is dead, so she does not have to see me like this. Raw, splayed to the bone ... empty.

◇◇◇◇◇

Voices rise in the mist. I am gripping the wood in a way that forces ivory marbles from my knuckles for fear of slipping into the scene below. From the cracks, I make out wavering shadows, the sound of laughter and little toes pounding across soft earth. It is only out of practice I can detect their movements beneath the growing sound of my heart beating.

Soon. Soon. Soon.

◇◇◇◇◇

It began suddenly. Grief provided an opening, and at my weakest point, Baba soiled the tip of his dagger. I can see now that he was always conditioning me long before we lost her. Quiet moments revealed hidden manipulations. Times he must have savored enfolding my younger self within his soft, slumping shoulders and whispering manifestations instead of words.

I would lean against his chest, my hair tickling the bottom of his chin, and listen to the unchanging lesson.

"You must be a hero, Arpita. In a world as unfair as ours, it is one's duty to tip the balance."

After Mummy's death, Baba taught me how to spot weaknesses. He showed me where to point my weapon, and at what moment to deliver the blow. I thought it was a distraction. Some way to harness the helplessness that he had felt in her death. He could not fight her disease and so he would fight the world instead. Delusions. As his love for her melted into madness, and he made the serum.

I did not know at first what had captured his attention. Watching him escape sleep for weeks on end, I thanked the gods for his absence. I assumed he was in prayer, healing on his own. Foolish. So unutterably foolish. I am not one to believe in Fate, but if it is out there, how I would *burn* every cell of it for what happened to me.

◇◇◇◇◇

I see them. A group of no more than three, wrapped tightly in charcoal garments. They rise over the sloping hills and collect in fluid, sinuous shadows jutting against the lavender fields in stark contrast. Set, remorseless, deadly. Approaching with intensity, the men are doused in rain to no avail. My eyes are drawn to the poorly concealed weapons enfolded within their robes. The outline of an elongated blade and several other bulging entities reveal what I am sure are not welcoming gifts.

I can almost convince myself they are nothing, beg my body to turn around. The serum is not fooled so easily as the rain slows in opposition to my heartbeat. I feel my movements from a faraway distance. It is as if I am watching myself now perched on the wood, screaming. Anything, anything to make me stop, to *hear* myself again. With calculated precision, I can sense my body readying for descent. I am a machine, I am hollow. I am reaching from far, far away.

◇◇◇◇◇

Baba stabbed me. *Hard.*

I woke from nightmares only to stare one in the face. Eyes carrying the weight of his stale bed, bloodshot and crusted, he clutched an empty syringe. Drenched in darkness, the hand that had once protected me from shadows had now become one. An intensifying smile split vinous cracks up his lips, his body shaking with exhaustion. "It is done!" he choked. "You are going to be beautiful, Beti."

I am the most hideous creature alive.

It almost killed me. Days passed and I could hardly move my head. Forced into silent horror, I sat in helpless agony as Baba brought stew to my lips, washed my crippled limbs, and cleaned my waste. He made me a prisoner in my own mind, in my own body. I never knew what it felt like to suffocate until I was lying in my own bed, recoiling at my father's arm against mine. He had taken everything. I was to serve his purpose, and

I could do nothing but watch as cell by cell, nerve by nerve I was lost.

After one month, I learned to walk again. It took three until I was back to eating, clothing, and doing everything human again by myself. At first, nothing had changed. Besides, that is, an unfamiliar part of myself that yawned and stretched, tapping its claws against a hate so vast I couldn't breathe while thinking about it. But recovery was slow, and Baba was there every step of the way. At night he would hold me against his chest and whisper prayers into the tangled strands of my crow black hair. My mind went numb beneath his touch and my body, stiff with revulsion, weighed heavier than stone. Motionless and detached, I couldn't find it in me to fight. The fire that once had burned within me was gone, wrapped up by the serum and thrown into a deep part of myself I didn't remember how to find.

◇◇◇◇◇

The robed men are here now. I have slunk so low to the roof they do not even look twice in my direction. I am good at melting into shadows; they are the proper temperature for all my hate.

◇◇◇◇◇

It didn't take long for the serum to prove itself to Baba. He held no trace of worry as, shrieking in horror,

I found myself running into fires, scaling dilapidated buildings, and sparring with armed strangers. In the beginning, I was blessed with blackouts so thick they swallowed me into an inky death. I would awaken in my old room again, Baba wiping blood from my covers and mumbling with the sickly sheen of someone who stared into eternity for too long.

I would learn what he had injected me with was a serum that forces me to save people. My brain, violated and maimed, is coerced into sending its foul signals crawling down my spine until I am no more than its puppet, tangled and splayed against the endless ropes of what is morally good. There is no decision between right and wrong. There is only this disease and what it tells me to do.

I must protect others over and over until I am so wounded I pray there is no return. I pray the burn marks blistering my throat will choke me, that the dagger nestled into my skin sliced mercifully through my falsely beating heart. But Baba heals me. Again and again, over and over until I am fighting, saving others against my will. When I was little I fought monsters, but now I am the monster. There is no way to restrain myself, no way to resist as I hurdle toward danger, anguish staining my cheeks in salt-ridden trails.

Villagers call me a hero. Families have prayed to me as though I am a god. But I know what I am. I am carved out. I am a corpse of a human. Baba hated the world so much, for what it did to Mummy, for what it simply *was,* that he made me a weapon. In trying to save others, he has utterly killed me.

◇◇◇◇◇

One swift motion and they have kicked the door off its ancient hinges. Screams burble below in the chaos of confusion curdled to terror. The serum kicks in, my muscles lurching to save the family. It takes down my body in a fiery compulsion to stop the men from ravaging this blameless home. My head is swimming, drenched with rain, drowned in thought. The world swirls below me.

No ... not this time, no longer.

I will not give in. I will not be controlled. I have been broken for months, but never have I felt this angry—this strong. Below, furniture snaps and crunches against the walls. Blurs are struggling, little voices screeching, but all else is lost to my senses in the pain. Every ounce of my flesh is on fire. Short, shallow breaths erupt from my lips as I clench myself against the soft fleshy timber. Searching for anything else to focus on, my eyes sink into the scars lacing my arms.

Unhealed gashes paint a gallery on my wrist, and just like Baba's weapons, they hold no resemblance to art. Catgut thread is frayed and scrunched against my puckering blood unearthed at the hand of an assassin's steel. I do not remember the family I saved that night, but the way my feet became bricks in the cold and blistered in voracious bumps. The dark pooling bruise engulfing my left forearm is a mere backdrop against the memory of earning it. The way I'd felt every bone in my body shudder when the thief pushed me up against rock. My father's betrayal fuels me, beads of sweat sprouting from my brow. I can hear the rapid pulsing of my heart; my hands are white against the slats.

A visceral scream sounds from beneath my chest. I cannot do it. I am going to either give in or self-combust. Ice is burning a trail through my veins. I bite into my arm to keep from yelling, my vision blurring in a cherry haze as I realize blood is trickling from my eyes.

Then, there is the hurried tempo of retreating footsteps, the trio making its way back across an ocean of grass. I cannot see much, but I do not think the blood in my eyes has colored the shade of red on their blades. I wait until they are out of view before relaxing my body. A guttural scream emits from my mouth, and I collapse through the roof, no longer able to hold myself back. Slamming into the ground, I feel nothing. The room shivers around me as I am shaking too violently to stand.

There is blood everywhere.

Speckled on the walls, dripping from the family table, licking every inch of soil. I glance down to find my stomach and legs covered in it. Stamped into my skin, it seeps through my clothes.

I force my eyes to look.

There is a little boy, no more than nine, unnervingly still in the corner. His head tipped back as if in prayer, dark lashes bowed beneath the weight of no reply. I do not linger long before the shape of a girl captures my attention beside the sodden table. She is too grotesque to understand, too red to comprehend anything else. Somewhere below me, my legs creak into an unsteady rise. My stomach lurches up and down, back and forth with every sluggish step. Dunked in ice, my brain has grown deftly silent as I step on something soft and hear the mangled crunch of human bones.

A woman's hand. Soft, gentle—still, much too still. Without consent the limbs below me convulse and lower. Solid earth hits my knees, my hand reaching toward hers, fingers outstretched, open. I can see the dirt stain beneath her nails, the curved lines tracing tallies down her palm. My fingers are inches from hers and suddenly, I am a snake again, lunging to capture time.

Then I hear the scream. It pierces the air behind me as, in one trained fluid motion, I am twisting a dagger from its cover and positioned for battle.

A man. A Baba. Baba.

He is hunched over and wailing blindly. Blood seeps from the inflicted wound laid into his shoulder as he screeches that he cannot move his legs. He is paralyzed from the waist down. I stalk toward him. His eyes meet mine and I can see the shimmer of sickening hope sweep across them. "Help! Help, you must help." For the first time he seems to be taking in the room. His gaze, unable to run, fixates on the bodies, on his family. Another guttural scream. I think he might pass out but he doesn't; instead voice cracking, he continues his plea. "Please, my fam—my family needs help. You must help us!"

I *must* help them. No.

That may once have been true, but not tonight, not anymore. Not after what I was just able to do. If I squint hard enough, I can believe this man is my Baba. Grey hairs peppered among the black. Heavy eyelids droopy from stress, ridden with plaintive lies. It is clear he is not, with his small frame and unfilled belly, yet I cannot help but hear Baba's voice.

Baba would insist that I save him. The serum would force my hands to his side. Yet here I exist, arms reaching toward him, fingers cradling a blade.

Realization stabs at his senses.

"No! Please!" It is useless; he is nothing but innocence blocking my way. Anger surges through me in a wave of nausea and awe. A force releases my mind. It is as if the serum is sliding off with the rain; buried within my bloody tears it slinks into the ground. With unfamiliar grace I am grabbing his throat between my hands. My blade rises to the occasion and in the reflection I can see myself smiling now, greedily, drunkenly. His life ends swiftly, unfairly. And dripping from the handle of my knife—I taste freedom.

science fiction & fantasy

Darling, If You Loved Me, You'd Sell Your Soul to Hell

Ashley Binstock

Grade 12. Bishop Neumann Central High School, Wahoo, NE. Marisa Grady, Educator. Gold Key.

Portfolio Gold Key

When I first arrived in Hell, all I could think was how impossibly empty it was. My thoughts raced with buried images of my father. My father who spent his days on earth drinking his self-inflicted punishment for beating me like it was holy water instead of booze. I thought surely he had to be in Hell, and then to my horror, I *wished* it.

The ground stretched out languorously, with piercing shafts of jagged rock and snaking between them, a sluggish coal black liquid. Shattered family photos, unused baby toys, and undecipherable sunken objects churned within the void. Soft and pliable to the touch, foreign earth drowned my every step as if little fingers were pulling me lower. In the hot, sticky tug, my stomach clenched and twisted in disgust at their taunting whispers scratching leisurely at my earlobes.

"There is no bottom. There is only below."

An endless horizon pitched against the ashen sky, lighting a dim spotlight on the nothingness that expanded before me. No ridges, no mountains, no burning fire and brimstone. Only me, the fizzling rock beneath my calloused feet, and the solid heavy haze that filled my lungs with lead.

Then, I felt it. In a shattering surge of nausea and terror, Hell settled into my bones with a wicked snap. It arched along my spine and flushed my veins with venom until I collapsed in a mangled, burning knot of flesh. I don't remember how I howled, but he would tell me later how I did. How my piercing screech had, like a flame, drawn him toward my anguish. I wailed until vomit spewed from my mouth and blackness curled and numbed my vision. There was no rest in Hell, only fear and pain and a loneliness I'd never felt before. A loneliness so thick I felt it scrape against my skull and lick the interior of my heart until, like roadkill, my swollen insides were ruptured with the insatiable decay.

I would have stayed there for all of eternity crying blood and ash if I hadn't seen—*him*. Crimson shadows balanced on his shuddering wings and swirled into sloping points on each elongated vertex. Hard, rigid lines of muscle spanned across his naked torso, reaching from his serrated chest down to bloody half-moon claws. He was magnificent and morose. Every inch of his oily tendons seemed to pulse with agony. Not quite human and not quite animal, yet he was someone, if merely something in all the aching space.

"Please ... *please,*" I had begged. He swept his talons out and as they unraveled toward me, I allowed the rough grasp to enfold me within his glacial arms. He carried me.

I should have been afraid of him. I should have begged that his pincers shred me into a million pieces until my insides mixed with Hell and became one. But the opening was widening against my skin like frost, and the only thing I couldn't seem to be, was alone.

The outlines of a face were creased into his leathery skull, as if water was thrown onto a once carefully detailed canvas. Only the indent of what had been remained. Studying his unformed face, time danced before my eyes. I pushed myself against his chest anyway, ignoring the pockets and caverns of scars branded onto every square inch of flesh. Flying above the ebon sea, I allowed my eyes to flutter up and down until Hell granted me the gift of nightmares as they landed with a grievous thud.

◇◇◇◇◇

I felt a pull. The moment I had risen to find earth mirrored above me was the same moment I understood there was a place I had to go. Some last appointment my soul was scheduled to attend. My body simply obeyed the lure, and when the demon planted my toes back on ember, they took me in the direction of the call.

"Where are we going?" I asked, half expecting no answer. The response rippled and drowned my senses in extinguishing thought.

To the gates. To the eternal gates.

"Why?"

So there is nothing of you left. So when they see you, they will see nothing.

We trudged along the unseen trail until my voice found a way to whisper, "Is that what you are? Nothing?" The answer shivered against my mind.

Yes.

Nothing couldn't have wings. Nothing couldn't crawl beside me on its spidery limbs. Nothing couldn't lift me up and carry me across Hell. Perhaps I was more like my father than I had ever realized.

◇◇◇◇◇

Surely it had been weeks. Weeks of crawling—I crawled now—across the barren tar pit. We didn't fly anymore. When I asked him why, his only response had been to cock his head and sink those hollow pits into me. Eyes or not, I didn't tremble when they surveyed me with the gaze of someone dissecting their next victim. I knew to the depth of my core I wasn't one. What sort of victim is thrown into Hell?

On especially tiring days, I curled up against him and we nestled into hidden craters. In his sticky, capsizing embrace I heard myself confess all the horrible ways my life had turned and the dreams I'd let slip through the cracks. He never spoke, not a single word, but in the heat he'd stroke his talons through my hair until my face softened to clay beneath his touch. It hurt less to not have expressions. I felt protected behind the mottled screen between myself and darkness. Only my breath mingled with the shadows, and I couldn't find it in me to mind when the clay hardened, and my hair floated in tangled webs straight through the ground.

I did not sleep again. Didn't seem to need to anymore. My limbs had stretched in an unnaturally gangly way and melted into a dull shade of gray. Days wore on, and I stopped thinking about Hell. I didn't see the corrugated earth as horrifying but simply where my feet shot out from. The shuddering breaths beside me reminded me I was not forgotten.

I wish I could say his presence grew on me. It didn't. He was hideous and cruel and unsettling in every way. Blood would spontaneously dribble down his chin, stalagmites popped up along his limbs. When he peered over and caught me looking, he would contort his head around his body until a splintering crack sounded in his neck and spiders crawled out of porous bumps along his skull. I would tumble away, vomit until my stomach clenched, and go on as if nothing had happened.

But that wasn't the worst of it. The worst was when he disappeared. When he left me alone in the nothing. My insides would freeze over and ache as a searing white heat rose to my head. It was as if I was pinned on a platter, watching from above as the view of me shrunk beneath a galaxy. Until I was no more than a shriveled insect, trivial and unseen. Perhaps that's why I learned to love his presence. Why I waited for him on all four paws.

I tell myself it's why I didn't care. Why I didn't so much as scream when colossal sinewy wings broke free from my back, digging two vertical train tracks down each side. Silent tears slid down my cheeks, but nothing within me stirred when he grabbed me by the waist and hoisted us into the sky. The sky with a limit. The sky that was pooling ink and roaring torture as my wings convulsed to life.

The atmosphere tapered off into a wall of black glass and I yelled, "Why does it have to hurt? Flying ... why does it feel so *wrong?*" His wings ground against mine until I understood the command to move. My soul had a place to be. A place that felt pointless now to appear.

Weight. You have become an incredible weight.

I surveyed the chalky legs below me, my claws curling up in pain. Flying was for the light, and I was the heavy scrape of a coffin taking its place beside worms.

◇◇◇◇◇

We arrived. Half descending, half plummeting toward rock in the chaotic thrashing of my wings. My chest collided with sludge, unsteadily slamming into the coiled river. My back went taut at the fiery stench of melted tar. Shrieking, I drug myself out of its burning tendrils and rolled over the edge onto solid ground. I clawed at the remaining splotches that left blisters the size of baseballs against my ribs. The demon landed beside me, entranced by something on the horizon. He took no notice of the way my ribs stuck out like the spiral of a notebook or how my leathery skin grew rosebuds of blood. I turned.

Clouded in ivory ringlets that danced in the outskirts of her form, she approached. A shimmering incandescent light. Her pure silken dress touched base around her waist, then flew out in feathery fragments that hovered above the earth. The not-earth that transformed into powdered snow footprints upon her touch. Her face was distinguished, with piercing hazel eyes and hair the color of cocoa. Strong jaw, golden freckles trailing both cheeks, and a shy nose.

Her figure wavered in the dark as if every cell of what she really was had been reined in for our consideration.

I pictured the thread holding her true form being severed and knew my soul would drown in that light. I could hear the beating of my phantom heart as she drew closer. My brain rattled with the inaudible snarls emitted from the demon, but even he did not pull away as she stepped onto my path.

"Hello, my dear." Her voice splintered the icy silence, my eardrums aching in the sound of air and lungs. How long had it been since I'd heard something? Had I not just released a shriek of my own? The angel's expression contorted in overt sympathy, and I wondered if she was taking in my appearance or reading my thoughts like the pages of an abandoned book. Suddenly, my insides contorted in her pity, and I lunged.

Slashing with brute strength and chiseled claws, my body collided with open air and slammed into the ground with a glorious thud. My vision turned black for two seconds before, crawling onto my feet, I unleashed a roaring hiss. Saliva sprayed and stuck in filmy clumps on the outstretched rock. I knew what this was, felt it to my core that somehow even Hell had granted me a second chance, and I had failed it.

Too late.

The serpentine voice sliced across my mind like the cut of an iron blade. No, not his voice. *Mine.* My voice was cracked lightening slipping through consciousness. And I felt nothing. The angel's enduring gaze latched on to mine, and I sniffed the disgusting aura of sorrow leaching from her pores.

Enough! I do not need your pity! I do not want to see your tears. I am ash and pain and misery. This air glides through my lungs in long luxurious breaths because I belong here now! I am a single cell of this flaming death. I am nothing.

To my horror, the angel's detailed expression softened. She extended her wrist and with the graceful flick of her finger, burned the demon, *my demon,* into embers. The remaining dust hovered around me in the empty haze as I felt my lungs collapse with a resounding twist.

In the fading glow she placed herself before me. "Now, my dear. Now you have chosen to be nothing. But once you were so alone you asked a demon to hold you. You whispered your hopeless dreams against its shadowed chest, grasped its talons between your forsaken palms, and allowed the darkness to fill the void." She was close now, so close her aura gnawed and bit into what was left of my damned soul. Leaching away any lost pieces of it that were left behind she breathed, "Once you were so strikingly human." In one fluid motion, she leaned in and pressed a kiss that liquefied in the sweat between my naked brows. With that, the angel glimmered and faded until nothing of her remained. A dull thud of light pounded against my forehead's leather skin, and when I eventually gathered enough strength to move, my legs shuddered in place. The ground had swallowed the lower half of my body as tiny frozen fingers plucked and tugged me lower ... lower.

Their cacophony of exultant voices rose against my chest as my ears plummeted toward their upraised voices.

There is no bottom. There is only below.

TALKING TO SHADOWS

ASHLEY BINSTOCK

Grade 12. Bishop Neumann Central High School, Wahoo, NE. Marisa Grady, Educator.

Portfolio Gold Key

Miguel hated the number two. It was the age he'd been when his mother plopped him down on the edge of his father's booze-stained rug and never looked back. Two was the number of years Miguel had been incarcerated. And worst of all, two was how many times each year he was forced to descend into one of San Francisco's particularly shaded alleyways, position himself against the balmy sun just right, and talk (yes, talk) to his shadow.

"¡Nia, vámanos! ¡No esperaré aquí para siempre!" Miguel grouched into the languorous reflection of his figure. Checking his watch, neon numbers flashed across his skin, spelling out how late she was. The charcoal outline of his shadow lounged against vermilion brick, looking particularly amused at his agitation. Miguel swore his 2D doppelganger had just stealthily clamped its hand over a stifled laugh when he heard her drawling voice.

"You know, people are going to think you're crazy if you keep talking to your shadow like that." He whirled to face her. Melting from the blood brick shadow, she glided out of a pool of ink. Suffocated in the swirling umbra, her lengthy limbs dipped in its dancing wisps, rising. Her eyes gleamed molten ivory as if spirits were trapped inside those huge hazel doorways. Finally, she surfaced. Miguel felt the air go out of him as her eyes returned their milky brown texture, and her umber skin loosed any remaining tendrils of shadow. He would never get used to the way she used shadows as a personal Uber. The way his heart defiantly stopped every time she settled back into a solid. "You know I don't understand you when you speak Spanish anyway." The sepia brown curls sloping in bubbles against her skin jostled as she approached him.

Miguel reclined into his usual scowl. "If you ever showed up on time, I wouldn't have to sacrifice my sanity by talking to a black mass of nothing." Instantly Miguel regretted saying anything, feeling the hard tug on his arm. His shadow, defying the stone boundary, ripped his limb into its black profile. He released a yelp as his flesh became smoldering ice, his arm lying dunked in the frozen silhouette. With a viscous shove, Miguel was freed from his shadow. Arctic vines bit along his pallid flesh, and frost bloomed until his arm looked like blue sky streaked with cirrus clouds.

Nia tsked slowly, "I'm afraid he did not like that comment, not at all." Gritting his teeth, Miguel watched his arm fade back to tan. With Nia, shadows had ears. They ran messages and allowed her to step slenderly out of them. With Nia, shadows could bite, and the San Francisco sun was the only thing brave enough to burn her powers away.

Bunching her hands into the side of her loose black jumpsuit, she shifted nervously on the gray wraps swirled around each foot. "You ready?"

No, was the simple answer.

Every unnatural, twisted thing in San Francisco would be crawling its way out of whatever gutter it had been living in to gather for the *bidding.* Hundreds of the city's gangs, cabals, businesses, and alliances Miguel didn't care to remember, swarmed like cockroaches into the pit to fight over what items the auction brought to the table. It was assumed among most that the government put it on as a great way to widen the city's wallet and encourage friendly competition. Of course, the latter held a long running tendency of blossoming into murderous feuds at an impressively fast rate.

Nia had been the one to suggest they start going three years ago. Not because they were a part of the maniacal cults, but because the auction had a habit of shifting power in the city. This way they could observe as alliances crumpled like wet paper and keep track of what groups rose in the food chain.

The hum of traffic hung over cement in the haze of an ending summer. Miguel's head tipped back, his hair slicing like black glass through the breeze. Everything in him wanted to forget about the scummy event. He ignored the familiar pit in his stomach that ached to turn around with Nia and never look back. Eventually, he breathed, "Twenty bucks there's a fight in the first four minutes."

Miguel felt the warm impact of Nia's hand against his as she pulled him into the dilapidated edifice. The last thing he saw was the soft arch of her smile descending into darkness and laughing. "Deal."

◇◇◇◇◇

Every kid savors losing their baby teeth. Grasping with pudgy, impatient fingers, they twist until the crimson block pops out for them to slip under their pillows and anxiously await its transformation into cash. For Nia, it happened all in one go, when the blast from her parent's meth lab exploding slammed her face first into the back of Grandma's wooden rocking chair. In some twist of luck, she had been in the farthest room from their "office" when the blowup occurred and had overall sustained minor injuries. But she still remembered coming to, her head aching like it had splintered into a million pieces and seeing *them*. Little pearly blood tipped teeth she had coughed up, lying like popcorn kernels on the carpet. She had turned seven the month before and, just like that, all those precious bargaining chips—gone. In less than a day she was hauled off to a foster home and spent the entirety of a summer squeezing Go-Gurts into her mouth. It was this particularly vivid memory that stuck to febrile summers ever since. That made her throat close up peering at the ivory pebbles peppered on that underground ceiling.

A cacophony of broken languages flew about the room like an out-of-tune piano as Nia took in the massive crowd. Tunnels from surrounding buildings all channeled into the circular arena, covering the span of a football field. Intense lights illuminated the suffocating crowd of people, some human, others not as much. She felt herself inspecting the cluster of shadows, escape routes unintentionally forming in her mind. The usual tense, electric energy stiffened in the air. Miguel and Nia slid against the back wall as a masked figure held court.

Standing on center stage, the man motioned for objects to be brought up as the bidding had already begun. Hands bobbed into the earthen sky, multiplying as items grew in power. Hexes capable of poisoning bloodlines, coordinates of secret arsenals, and so on until the words blurred together in the hypnotic rise of palms. Out of the corner of her eye, Nia found more entertainment watching scrutinizing grid lines crease into Miguel's bronze complexion. Finally, after what felt like a lifetime, the auctioneer boomed, "And our last object up for bid tonight." His velvet maroon suit looked like it was cut from Victorian drapes, waving for the final object to be revealed. Nia's shoulders straightened against the dirt wall. She felt the air calcify at the bottom of her lungs.

A little girl, no more than six, was forced onto the dais. Numbing silence engulfed the crowd as the girl's expression flashed across the cascade of people sinking their eyes into her. Horror wrinkled the smears of dried dirt pressed against her cheeks. Her auburn hair lay tangled in unwashed clumps dangling above her collarbone. "Watch closely," the masked figure commanded. He thrust out his hand, gripping the little girl's wrist as she struggled. Clasping onto her, he turned their interlocked arms toward the audience. Nia dug her fingernails into the fabric of her pants. Creeping ashen splotches embedded into the man's arm, decay spreading like wildfire up his flesh. Pieces broke off and floated to the floor, deteriorating into dust before flattening against the ground. Maggots sprouted from exposed crevices, his arm transforming into a rotting corpse as the girl's eyes grew to the size of empty saucers. In one fluid motion, the man tore away with a hiss. Slowly, the decay dissipated, maggots shriveling out of existence and supple living cells unfurling across his flesh.

"Miguel ..." Nia's voice sounded distant, distorted in the uproar of hungry cries, chanting for more. They had never gone this far. Never auctioned off a person, let alone a *child*.

A child with power over death.

Nia stared at Miguel. At the sharp curve of his jawline drawn tight with unease, his almond bark eyes darkening at the sight. He arched one eyebrow, as though if he focused hard enough the bushy arrow would fire straight into the heart of every repulsive being willing to enslave a six-year-old.

"I know," he rumbled. It would be ridiculous, downright stupid of them to attempt to steal her. A chamber full of not-so-human people willing to shake the walls apart for a little girl who could topple the balance of power. Trying to take her would be suicide. But there was something in her terrified stare. Something that reminded Nia of a little boy with black shaggy hair and a t-shirt that smelled like his father's beer can. Something that prickled every nerve in her body, thinking of holding that boy's hand and feeling like she never wanted to let it go. A nostalgic wave of emotions that settled her decision. "Tell me we can't do it," Miguel whispered, reading her thoughts.

Nia shook her head as their eyes met in the sweltering chaos.

"Thought you might say that."

◇◇◇◇◇

The tunnel's odor was an overwhelming concoction of urine and rat feces, a mosaic of ceiling tiles scattered in piles along the floor. After scoping out the emptiest escape route, Miguel had found one leading straight into a rundown basement. The dirt tunnel opened into an underground hallway where it took Miguel all of three minutes to knock out one guard with an old door handle as the thunderous bidding continued below. Violence had broken out after the last auction item performed her how-to-build-a-zombie tutorial, forcing the auctioneer to usher the kid out of the arena. Nia was somewhere within the fold, most likely leap frogging from shadow to shadow, searching for her as Miguel leaned all of his weight against another guard, pinning him against the wall. The guard was an unwarrantedly hairy man, maybe fifty, with a buzz cut of silver hair that protruded from every square inch of exposed skin in course spindles. Squirming against Miguel's grip, he yelled in protest. Miguel released a deep breath, preparing for what he had to do.

He would never forget the screams he heard the first time he used his ability. The way the human face could stretch like taffy, slackened with too much weight. Miguel heard that same cry now, the man lurching in spasms against his touch as he cracked open the guy's mind like a soda can and seeped his soul inside the cracks. It had felt like drowning the first time; now Miguel wrangled the images and broken thoughts flashing like strobe lights through the foreign mind efficiently, stashing everything the man was into a box deep inside his being. The guard's eyesight cleared. Miguel faced his real body, torn jeans and vacant eyes penetrating the hands pushed up against his temporary form. He could see the lines of sweat trailing beneath the black edges of his hair, watched as they jumped to the floor.

As he scoured the man's knowledge for what other problems they might bump into, the sound of gunshots shattered his concentration. A wave of nausea swam through the older, unfamiliar chest as he pictured Nia somewhere below them. Forcing himself to refocus, he gathered useful pieces of information embedded in the man's brain. He was steadying himself to slip back into his rightful body when a blur broke through his vision.

Nia.

Unharmed, unfazed Nia standing with her arm bracing a rail-thin girl. Relief flooded Miguel's system, a rippling, unnatural grin breaking the surface of his borrowed features. It must have looked as grotesque as it felt as Nia's hazel eyes widened and she uttered, "Don't ever do that again."

Miguel relaxed his hold on the man's mind, slamming back into his own body. He crumpled to the ground, the guard dropping like a potato sack alongside him. Miguel peered at the grotesque waves of flesh protruding from the man's face and quickly looked away as he called, "No posts past this point. Gunshots?"

"In the pit, not by me." Nia motioned to the girl. "I found her in a sealed off vault inside the walls." She looked even thinner up close, a thick layer of grime buried into every open patch of skin. An amount of filth that couldn't have accumulated in one night. "You alright?"

Miguel watched Nia's gaze dart between him and the slumped over figure flattened against the wall. Glancing down, he noticed the slow trickle of blood trailing down his fingertips in what must have fallen from the man's nose. "Fine. But we won't be if we don't get out of here, now."

Nia nodded tersely. She turned, lowered herself to a kneeling position, and gently traced her hand down the girl's face until it curled around her pointed chin. "We're going to get you out of here, okay?" The kid did little more than nod blankly when Miguel rose to his feet and Nia held onto her pint-sized palm. The three of them turned, sprinting toward the end of the domino-tiled hallway. Miguel's heartbeat felt like a weight pounding divots into his chest. He thought of his long-engrained hatred for running, the hallway horizon seeming to stretch away from them with each second. Miguel could make out the stone fossil of a staircase looming toward the bottom of a metal door no more than thirty yards away. His feet pounding promises into the floor that they were getting closer ... and closer.

But then Miguel felt it.

He felt it like fire in his chest. He felt it like electric shocks ricocheting inside his lungs long before he ever heard the gunshot. The room blurred. His every nerve crystallized and shattered, watching Nia plunge to the floor beside him. Everything in him was burning as he collapsed to the ground, wrapping his arms around her waist and turning her limp body to face him. He was screaming. Surely, he sensed some distant part of himself shouting to the stars as he forced his hands against the wound. Blood gushed from the hovering warmth of her flesh in a wall of red. Miguel wiped her soft curls behind her ears in a stroke of blood. His fingertips shook against the dark arch of her neck, searching for a pulse. A pulse that didn't exist. A pulse he would have sold his soul for. Icy stinging tears sliced down his cheeks and fell in shards of glass to Nia's hair.

"She's too beautiful to die."

The little girl was kneeling next to him, gazing at Nia's lifeless form as she imitated the way Nia had caressed a gentle line down her own face earlier. She repeated as if in a trance, “She’s too beautiful to die.” The rushing sound in Miguel’s head subsided enough to realize someone was yelling at him.

“Step away from the girl.” An entourage of armed guards pointed their weapons. The masked auctioneer stood behind them saying, “Just because we shot your friend doesn’t mean you have to die too. Now. Hand. Over. Our. Girl.”

Miguel scowled, his lips curling in disgust realizing the only reason he wasn’t dead, was because the kid was covering him. Her body blocked his hunched over form, constructing too risky of a shot for them to take. That is unless they were willing to blow their auction item’s brain out.

Miguel felt a light nudge on his arm. The girl remained bent over Nia; lowering her eyes she whispered, “Help her up. I don’t accept her.”

“What?” he choked.

“She’s still here. I won’t take her.”

Miguel’s heart dunked through the bottom of his chest as the hand twisted around Nia’s waist rose in a shuddering breath.

◇◇◇◇◇

It had been over in an instant.

One second they were running, her padded feet like quiet thunder, racing to the end of that hall. She had been so distracted. She couldn't even hear her own shadows whispering to her. *Turn. Turn. Turn.* A few seconds of agonizing pain crashed through her before the descent to that ungodly tile.

But now she saw him. From miles away, as if she were looking through a distorted mirror, trying to assemble an image from all the warps. She tumbled, swirling upward until—light. Nia barely registered Miguel's hands around her torso, rotating in his grasp. She planted her fingers firmly on the ground, her eyes carving through the group of guards whose gazes shifted in fear at what she was. At what she wasn't supposed to be anymore. "Friends?" Her voice carried across the hallway, finding each one of their shadows in harmony as one by one the group was plucked into their own shadows' ink stains against the floor.

They vanished, pulled into the relentless void, to an unforgiving Hell. After a breath, their shadows released them. The men, women, and monsters alike popped above ground shaded in baby blue, their veins bulging like icicles against pulseless throats.

"Nia ..."

Nia turned toward the beacon. Toward her boy with black shaggy hair. He was smiling, the crooked thing curling shamelessly across his cheeks. She reached toward him, pulling the girl against her chest. The girl who rejected her soul from death. "I never liked San

Francisco," Nia breathed. Miguel nodded, understanding passing between them at what they had done. At all the reasons they couldn't stay.

"Me either." And they ran.

This Is Not a Test: Dox-77

Katie Bough

Grade 10. Northwest High School, Grand Island, NE. Natalie Starostka, Educator. Silver Key.

This is it. This is the end.

These were the thoughts that raced through my head as I backed into the corner of Mr. Wilson's Advanced Chemistry class as the horde of zombies closed in.

Okay. That was the hook. Are you hooked? Okay, cool. Sooo ... I probably need to explain how I got into this situation in the first place. Okay. Um. Let's go back a little bit.

It was early October. Everything in the world was pretty chill, you know, relatively speaking because the world is always kind of insane, but there weren't, like, any world wars raging or mass hysteria going on at the moment. Of course, unbeknownst to us (us being almost the entire population of the world), some idiot scientists at a lab in Roswell, New Mexico had just released a deadly strain of the virus Dox-77 upon the world. They were trying to find a cure for migraines but instead accidentally created an unprecedented airborne killing machine. I mean, come on! You had *one job!* That's like, someone asks you to do the dishes and gives you $20 to just try to do the dishes and you smash the dishes on the floor, burn the house down, and overthrow the Albanian government. Ugh.

Anyway, they release this virus and don't even realize it until, oh holy moly macaroni! News reports start flooding in of people going cuckoo, not for Cocoa Puffs, but for human flesh! So the government is like, "Let's do some testing!" And the testing comes back with results for some virus they'd never seen before. So they alert all the companies that are researching some cure for some ailment and are like, "Stop what you're doing and research a cure for this right now or else. Love you!" And that one company that actually created the virus and didn't know it starts researching and realizes, "Oh fudgesicles, this virus is exactly identical to failed cure 77. Well, shucks." So, probably trying to avoid being shut down by the government and skinned alive by the general public, they destroy all the records of their research and rebrand themselves as aromatherapy acupuncturists: The Future of Modern Medicine! At this point, the rest of the world doesn't care much because their neighbors and dentists and nieces and nephews are trying to eat the skin off of their faces.

So I know I used the word "zombies" in the second paragraph, but I suppose I should explain what that actually means. You see, there are the zombies in the books, movies, shows, and comics that you know about, the emaciated creatures that thirst for b-b-brrraaaaaiiiiinnnss. But the zombies infected by the Dox-77 virus are not picky eaters. Brains are good but so are arms, index fingers, earlobes, anything really. And these zombies don't need to be dead first or be bitten to become a zombie. The Dox-77 virus is highly contagious. It can be transmitted through air, through touch, through water, etc. The virus impairs thinking and causes an infected person to become delirious, delirious enough to believe flesh is their new favorite food. The virus wreaks havoc on their immune system, their reaction time, and their brain functions. If you are infected, you are not dead. But you are slowly dying.

Alright, now that we got all that background information out of the way, let's get into the actual story. Like I said, it was early October. I lived in Bloomington, Indiana, which meant sometimes in the morning it would get so foggy it felt like you were in a haunted house and the kid in control of the fog machine forgot how to turn it off. I was a sophomore at West Hill High School. On October 7th, I was half asleep in Mrs. Turner's Spanish class. It was the last class of the day, and I had it right after Algebra so there was about a 2% chance that I would actually make it through the class without falling asleep. I eluded getting in trouble because I did my work and didn't cause any problems in class, which some of my classmates seemed to struggle with. Don't get me wrong, it is pretty entertaining to watch the boys squabble over who can benchpress more in Strength Training, but I just want to go to school, do my work, and get out. And that's pretty hard to do when there has to be a lecture each class period about paying attention and being respectful and how this sh*t ain't gon' fly in college so you better get your act together now, you hear me? Yeah.

So, Mrs. Turner was going on about affirmative informal commands and conjugating verbs until—thank the Lord—the bell rung, liberating us and saving our last bit of sanity. I snapped out of my sleepy spell and began to gather my supplies and place them back in my bag. Getting up, I said goodbye to Mrs. Turner and began the trek to the parking lot. The exodus of high school students stampeded through the school and toward the exits like always. I succeeded in not getting trampled, at least not today. While walking down the hall, I spotted my friend Dallas ahead of me; he was always easy to spot, being that he was freakishly tall. He had golden blonde hair and a little baby mustache that I was always trying to convince him to shave, but he refused to because it's his "man 'stache" or something like that. He had pretty brown eyes, like chocolate mixed with caramel. He was a little chubby, but I couldn't judge. My mom calls my body "womanly," my friends call my body "curvy," and I call my body "ew." I'd often lament exceedingly about how much I disliked how I looked until Dallas told me, "shut up or I'll steal your teeth."

I picked up the pace and began moving hurriedly down the hall. Once I reached Dallas I tapped his right shoulder and started walking next to him on his left side. He looked around for a moment and then spotted me walking alongside him.

"Did you just tap me on the shoulder?" he said.

"Nope. Nuh-uh. Not me," I replied.

"That's funny. Could've sworn someone tapped my shoulder like two seconds ago. Weird."

"Maybe you're going crazy. Personally, I wouldn't be surprised."

"Even if I did go crazy, I would never be able to reach your level of crazy. By the way, that's not a good thing."

"Hey! Watch your tone young man or I *will* have to annihilate you. Some of us have feelings, you know."

"Yeah, sensitive little baby feelings ..."

At this point, I stomped on his foot, which, since he was wearing steel-toed boots, he was already prepared for. Totally unfair. We continued to walk through the school until we reached the main entrance where we waited. He could drive, but he waited with me for my Dad to pick me up before driving home. This month, though, my parents were on vacation in Hawaii so my grandma was picking me up. He had offered to drive me home many times but I told him my confidence in his driving skills was minimal at most. Really, I just didn't want to bother him by making him drive me home. He had said it really wouldn't be a bother to him, but I don't know, he might've just been saying that.

At this point in time, we knew that there was an issue going on in New Mexico with "zombies." But since everyone had been assured that the issue was contained in New Mexico, we were still allowed to go to school. Honestly, most people thought the whole zombie thing was a hoax. Some had started to stock up on provisions though, just in case. As we were waiting, the tornado sirens came on. Which wasn't totally unusual but quite strange considering there wasn't a cloud in the sky and the wind was hardly blowing. A few teachers came to usher the students back inside. While the siren's plaintive sound continued, every phone in the vicinity went off at the same time with the same urgent beeps. Dallas and I glanced at each other and then checked our phones. All around us, there were gasps and murmurs as we read the emergency alert on our screens:

EMERGENCY ALERT
THIS IS NOT A TEST

The Dox-77 virus is no longer contained in New Mexico. It has spread to the following states: Arizona, Arkansas, Colorado, Illinois, Indiana, Kansas, Louisiana, Missouri, Nebraska,

> Oklahoma, Texas, and Utah. Stock up on resources, prepare an emergency kit, review first aid techniques, seek immediate shelter. For further information, visit www.emergencyalertusa.gov.

"Ho-ly sh*t," whispered Dallas.

The agitated chorus of voices around us increased in volume. The cool autumn air was now fraught with fear.

Just then I got a text from my Mom. It read, "Haley, have you seen the news? The Dox-77 virus has spread. We're coming home immediately. Go straight home and protect yourself. I love you so much, sweetie."

Another text, this time from my grandmother. This one read, "They've quarantined the college, we're stuck here until everyone is tested and cleared. I can't come to pick you up. I'm so sorry. Do not take the bus or hitchhike, any stranger might have the virus. See if that nice boy can take you home since you've already been around each other long enough that if he was sick by now you would be sick too. Stay safe, I love you darling."

My grandmother worked at the community college as an Adult Education teacher. There were people constantly going in and out of the building. No wonder they had quarantined it. A lump in my stomach began to grow with dread. I felt completely helpless. Dallas wore a grimace on his usually cheerful face.

"We have to get out of here," he said in an urgent tone.

I nodded numbly and walked hastily with him to his truck. We jumped in, threw our backpacks into the backseat, and buckled our seatbelts. Dallas started the car and sped out of the parking lot. He started talking quickly.

"Okay, so the virus has spread. We need to prepare ourselves. You're going to stay with me. It's going to be mayhem at the stores. We'll drive to your house and collect all the supplies we need. Then we'll go to my house and make camp there." He seemed to be talking more to himself than to me.

"But my parents! They're coming back, and—and I need to be at home! I can't just—" I tried to organize my jumbled thoughts.

"Soon enough all airports in America will be shut down in an attempt to contain the virus. Your parents will be stuck in Hawaii. They'll be fine. As of right now, the virus is only in America. Your house is in the middle of town, surrounded by other houses and stores, meaning, surrounded by other people. If the virus hits town, it'll spread like wildfire. If you're at your house, you'll be right in the middle of it," he reasoned.

"But—" I tried to argue back.

"My house is out in the country, we have no neighbors for miles. Only a few people even know where my house is. My dad is a survivalist junkie, he has been preparing for something like this to happen for years. We have a bunker, supplies, and the knowledge to get us through this. You have to trust me."

He was right. At my house, I was a sitting duck. We had a pantry downstairs with some cans of soup and cereal, but that was it. We didn't have any weapons, I had no idea how to give CPR or tend to a wound or make a fire, and my house was right in the middle of town. Dallas had been hunting for years. His whole family was a bunch of survival experts. He knew how to use a gun, a knife, a bow and arrow, and I had seen him fight at school before. Freshman year he was really angry. He never spoke in class. He would show up with scraped-up hands and bruises on his face. People liked to whisper about him. "*I heard his mom's a drunk.... I heard his dad got laid off....*" I never spoke in class either. People used to call me "mouse," mostly because they didn't know my name, but they did know that I was quiet as a mouse. One day, in science class, Aiden Sihger was in a particularly bad mood. He was a prominent figure in the hierarchy of high school, one of the louder boys, he always had something to say. He wasn't the brightest or biggest, but he was fearless, and that made people fear him. Dallas was in that class and so was I. Aiden was looking for someone to pick on, someone to break. I was the quiet girl, I never spoke and I most definitely never spoke up for myself. The teacher was out of the room, he had gone to the library to look for some copies he had made last period. Aiden decided to have some fun.

He pulled my hair. Not a playful tug, he yanked my hair back and my neck went with it. It didn't break or anything, but I heard something crack.

"Ow!" I yelped.

"Oh! So you can speak?" he said with a sneer. Kids all around the room were snickering.

I felt my face grow hot and my eyes started to tear up. I just stared at my desk and prayed it would be over soon.

"Hey! I'm talking to you. Are you mute and deaf too? F*cking r*tard," he said. The boys at his table were laughing louder now.

"The f*ck did you just call her?" said Dallas. His eyes were bright and dangerous.

"I called her r*tard, r*tard. What? Does that offend you? You special little snowflake," Aiden said in a mocking tone.

Dallas got up from his chair and in two steps he towered right over Aiden. Aiden stood up quickly. All around the room, there were murmurs of "Oooh ..."

"Does this offend you?" asked Dallas as he slammed his fist into Aiden's face.

With one punch, Dallas had broken Aiden's right cheekbone and knocked out his upper right canine tooth. Dallas was suspended for two weeks.

So he could fight, and I didn't know how to make a fist. His house was perfectly safe out in the country with no neighbors, and mine was in the middle of town. He was prepared, and I was not. The choice was obvious.

"Okay, I trust you," I said at last.

Boy was I in for one wild apocalyptic ride.

Treacherous Stars

LOGAN SYLLIAASEN

Grade 11. Bishop Neumann Central High School, Wahoo, NE. Marisa Grady, Educator. Silver Key.

An alarm blared to life, stirring me from my sleep. *They've found me,* I thought, panicking. *I didn't even make it out of this planet system.* But even the fate I'd face on this starship was better than the past I had left behind.

Boom.

An explosion rocked the ship, and the five other girls in my cabin jumped to their feet, looks of confusion and fear mingling with grim determination as they pulled on simple black security uniforms. Attempting to push aside my paranoia, I rushed to follow suit, strapping my standard issue blaster into the holster at my thigh. I turned and began to file out the door with the others, just as we had been trained.

My foot caught on the untied lace of my other boot, and I pitched forward, straight into the girl in front of me. "Sorry—" I began as she turned to look at me, her nose wrinkled in disgust.

"Get off of me!" she sneered, shoving me. I started forward, my blood thrumming with the possibility of a fight, but a hand grabbed my shoulder, pulling me back.

"Let it go, Taryn," Eden, my assigned shift partner, muttered before turning toward the other girl with a glare. "Don't you have bigger things to worry about than your pride right now, Rori?" she said, her voice firm with authority.

Rori huffed and turned away, flipping her dark hair over her shoulder.

The ship hallway was awash in varying shades of gray as we marched, listening intently to the beat count from the blaring alarm.

Two rings, followed by a single long, shrill note. Panicked whispers spread through our ranks as the alarm sequence sounded over and over. We all knew what it meant. *Irreparable damage in quadrant two. All personnel report to the hangar bay for immediate evacuation.*

Explosions near the engine quadrant of star ships certainly weren't unprecedented, but something about this wasn't right. Prior to takeoff, when my forged documents were approved and I was admitted to the security team, I had been informed that our ship would be transporting an undercover high-profile ambassador who had been hounded by kidnapping and assassination attempts on her home planet and had needed immediate extraction. I was also informed that she would be disguised as a security guard in one of the squadrons in my barracks.

Suddenly, another massive *boom* rocked the ship, and a wave of heat flowed around us. I looked up to see a huge chunk of debris dislodge from the ceiling, and I watched in a daze as it fell toward me. A blur of motion from my left caught my eye, and I turned to see Rori crash into me, tackling me across the hall.

We rolled several times before skidding to a stop. I lay on my back, gasping for air, my ears ringing, as Rori struggled to her feet before offering me a hand. I stared at her in shock before taking it.

"Why would you do that?" I gasped, unable to keep the disbelief from my voice.

"It was the right thing to do," she replied with a small smile. "Don't let this go to your head, though. I still don't like you." She turned away from me to survey the damage.

The hall in front of us, the only way to reach the hangar, had collapsed, its walls blown in by the explosion.

We were trapped.

I turned to Eden, and I knew we were both thinking the same thing. This wasn't a simple engine malfunction. This was deliberate sabotage.

A burst of adrenaline tinged with excitement shot through me, and I wrung my hands in nervous energy as my eyes roved over our squad. Some were slumped in defeat, while others clawed at the rubble, trying to shift it enough to clear a path.

"Hey!" our leader Astrid, a tall, muscular girl with sharp eyes, shouted. "Everyone back in formation! This may not be an ideal situation, but we cannot just throw protocol out the window!"

Five pairs of eyes turned toward her, awaiting further instructions. "We'll head to the cockpit, and make our way to the hangar from there," she ordered.

"But all the escape pods will have launched already," Rori protested.

"Then we try to steer what's left of this ship toward safety," Astrid replied grimly, "And if we don't make it, at least we died trying. Now let's move!"

That was when the lights went out.

Several girls screamed, their voices piercing the darkness, and I took off, promptly abandoning the protocol Astrid had just preached to us about. Order was not our friend in this situation, but speed was. Light flickered at the very end of the hallway, and I pushed toward it, five pairs of boots pounding against the floor behind me in a race against time. We had to get into the cockpit before we lost all power. In an emergency, it was the only part of our ship with a backup store of oxygen and a substantial amount of emergency power. We weren't seeking an escape route. We were simply delaying the inevitable.

I flew around a corner and skidded to a halt outside the cockpit doors, Eden and Kora close behind. We turned and watched as Rori and Astrid followed, their breaths coming in gasps.

"Where's Bree?" Kora asked. "I thought she was right behind you guys."

"She was," Astrid replied, her expression puzzled. "I'm sure she's coming." She turned toward the doors with her hands on her hips. "How are we going to get these open? I don't have the clearance, and I don't think any of you do either."

"You might want to stand back." I pulled out my blaster and leveled it at the control panel. "I've always wanted to try this," I murmured, then squeezed the trigger. Nothing happened. Frowning, I shook my gun and tried again, bracing myself for a shot that never came.

The others drew their blasters and attempted to fire as well, but to no avail. More sabotage. I met the eyes of every girl around me, my brain flying through the possibilities, before tossing my blaster aside with a nervous chuckle.

"Must be a strange coincidence, huh?" I said with a grin that felt forced even to me. "Anyone else have a brilliant idea?"

"Step aside." Rori smirked, pulling out a gleaming silver clearance card. I sucked in a breath, my eyes narrowing.

"Where did you get that?" Eden asked.

"I nicked it off a chef a few days ago," replied Rori, spinning the card across her fingertips. "I just wanted a few extra snacks."

"And you didn't think to mention it until now?" Kora questioned, her eyebrows raised.

"What *matters* is now we can get into the cockpit." Rori stepped forward and tapped the card against the panel, grinning as it glowed green. She turned toward us as the doors slid open. "Now, how about a thank you?"

"Sure thing," I muttered, then shouldered my way past her into the cockpit and gasped.

Growing up in the criminal underworld of one of the largest cities in the known galaxy, I'd seen my fair share of bodies, and even helped create a few myself, but this was different. Five bodies, throats slit from ear to ear, were scattered across an otherwise pristine room. There were no blood splatters, no destroyed instruments, no sign of a struggle. For the first time tonight, a real sense of fear and foreboding slithered down my spine. Until now, I had seen this as an exciting adventure, a daring escape. I hadn't truly believed I was in any kind of danger. Somehow, I had thought, without a doubt, that I would find a way out of this. But now I knew better. This wasn't the work of some common criminal. This was a trained killer, an occupation I knew all too well.

A retching sound came from behind me, and I turned to see Kora heaving her dinner onto the floor while Eden and Rori stared at her with twin looks of disgust that I would have found comical in any other situation. Astrid leaned against the door, her face pale. Me, Kora, Eden, Rori, and Astrid. That was only five.

"Why isn't Bree here yet?" I hated the quiver in my voice, but even I couldn't hide my fear with bold confidence now. Four sets of eyes turned toward me before darting to the other faces around the room.

"Maybe there was someone in the hall, waiting to pick off stragglers," Eden suggested.

"Or Bree was the ambassador, and the assassin took her and left," Rori said. "Either way, I say we barricade ourselves in here and use the emergency power to make for the nearest planet."

"Oh yeah? With what? Our engine is a bit toasty, remember?" I shot, irritation clipping my voice. "Besides, the assassin could very easily be in this room right now, and is simply picking us off one by one. They could have grabbed Bree while the rest of us were running here, and when they realized she wasn't the ambassador, killed her to even the odds a bit."

"Right, then if you're so smart, who's the killer?" Rori asked mockingly.

"Well, you and Astrid were the last ones here, so you tell me."

Rori gasped at the accusation and drew herself to her full height. "I saved your life, Taryn. Would an assassin have done that?" she scoffed. "Astrid was behind me the whole time, and I thought I saw Eden pass us at one point."

"That's ridiculous. I was right behind Taryn the whole time!" Eden protested. "Astrid wanted us to come here in the first place, and she was the last one here. This was all part of her plan!"

They all shouted back and forth at each other, pointing fingers and screaming accusations that became increasingly unfounded. Kora slowly backed into a corner and crumpled to her knees, where she rocked back and forth, her arms wrapped around herself as she stared blankly out the window at the stars twinkling far, far away from us.

I walked toward the navigation console, drawn by a red light that continued to blink faster and faster. The blood drained from my face and I cursed. "You guys might want to see this."

"What is it?" Rori questioned as she walked toward me.

"We've been caught in the gravitational pull of a nearby star," I said, "and without an engine to fight it—"

"How long do we have?"

"30 minutes? Maybe 35 if we're lucky."

Rori sighed and ran a hand through her hair. "Don't worry, I—"

A strangled gasp sounded from behind me. I whirled, realizing I'd forgotten about the other three girls.

Astrid lay on the ground, blood pouring from a neat gash across her throat, nearly identical to the ones painting the necks of the pilots that lay around us. And, standing several feet from Astrid's body with a bloody knife pressed against Kora's neck, was Eden.

I realized several things at once. First, Rori, which probably wasn't even her real name, was the ambassador, which explained why she'd had a clearance card earlier. Second, Rori and I were about the same height and build, both with long dark hair and brown eyes, which lead to my third conclusion: Eden didn't know which one of us was the ambassador. All I had to do was blow Rori's cover, and I'd be free.

"I think you both know why I'm here, so I'm going to make this very simple for you," Eden said, a crazed glint in her eyes. I stared at her in shock. We'd slept in the same room together, shared shifts with each other, and I had never noticed anything off about her. I had been too caught up in my own worries to notice the killer right beside me.

"All I want is for Ambassador Elowen to turn herself over to me, and poor, innocent Kora here"—Eden dug her knife into Kora's throat, coaxing a few drops of blood from her skin—"will get to keep her pretty little head."

Ambassador Elowen? The name was certainly familiar to me. I'd spent my life seeing her image in magazines, her figure waving on screens, making empty promises to help my planet, a planet that had only brought me pain and misery.

Eden's eyes darted between us. "Well? I really haven't got all night. My bosses—" her face paled slightly, "will be here any time now, and they won't be pleased if I don't have their precious prize." She looked at us with increasing desperation, her chest heaving slightly, as neither of us moved. "You're really going to make me spill innocent blood over this? They're not even going to kill you anyway, Ambassador! You'll just be their pretty little puppet. And besides," she let out a deranged giggle, "we all become puppets eventually. It's only a matter of time. And if I don't complete this assignment," she let out a hysterical laugh, "my strings will become a noose."

I stood frozen, paralyzed. All I had to do was point, say a name, and this would all be over. Kora, Rori, and I would all live. But somehow, I couldn't bring myself to do it. I wouldn't sentence another girl to live a life of chains, a life manipulated by hands wreathed in shadows, not like the life I had escaped from. This had to be her choice.

I looked over at Rori. Her face was pale, her breath coming in short gasps. I could see the conflict written across her face. She opened her mouth, about to speak—

"You don't think I'll do it? I will, I really will!" Eden shrieked, raising the knife above her head.

"No, wait—" Rori shouted, but it was too late. Eden plunged the knife into Kora's chest, over and over and over again. A scream echoed across the cockpit, and it took me a second to realize it was mine as blood splattered across the navigation panels in a splash of scarlet. Kora let out a rattling gasp, then slumped to the floor, lifeless.

Eden stepped over the body, wiping at the blood painting her face with a single fist. She spread her arms wide and grinned shakily at us, red dripping from the knife still clutched in her hand. "Well?" she screamed. "Do you believe me now?"

I edged toward the seat where a pilot's body lay prostrate. If I could just reach his blaster—

Eden cocked her arm back, aiming the knife straight at me. "Not. Another. Step." I froze, my breaths coming in shallow pants.

Rori raised her arms placatingly and stepped forward. "Please, don't do this. Can we just talk?" That was when I noticed she had stepped closer to one of the bodies. All she had to do was reach slightly to her right to grab his blaster.

"Eden," I said, my hands shaking as I raised them placatingly. "My name is Taryn Rohdes. I used to be an assassin in the Remaliah Guild." Her eyes flicked toward me, and I saw the recognition there. "You know my name. I know what it's like to be trapped in that life, a life you didn't choose. But you can escape like I did! Just let me help you!"

"There is no escape, not from this." I saw Rori reach for the gun, and the world slowed as Eden's gaze was drawn by the slight movement. Her arm twitched, and suddenly I was moving, racing across the few feet separating Rori and me. Eden's wrist flicked, and her knife flew toward Rori. I dove, extending my body just as Rori glanced up, a blaster in her hand.

The blade buried itself deep into my stomach as I crashed to the floor. I heard a shot, and the limp thud of another body hitting the ground, and then Rori was on her knees beside me, her hands pressing into my stomach, trying to stop the blood flowing from around the tiny knife buried there.

"Why would you do that?" she asked, her eyes wild.

"It was the right thing to do," I gasped, echoing her words from earlier. "Besides, I owed you one."

I reached a weak hand toward Eden's limp body. Blood leaked slowly from the blaster wound on her forehead. "I could've helped her," I murmured, my heart breaking for a girl I thought I'd known.

Rori pulled off her jacket and wadded it up against my wound. I winced, but the pain felt distant. I was slowly going under, drowning as the pool of my blood rose higher and higher.

"Just hang on," she whispered. "There are people coming for me. They can help you. Just hold on."

I gazed up at the stars gleaming outside the cockpit, sparkling from thousands of miles away. A shadow fell over us as a massive ship glided in overhead.

"Help is almost here," Rori said, hope gleaming in her eyes. I heard footsteps echoing in the hall, voices shouting urgently, before a group of heavily armed soldiers burst in.

"I need a medic!" Rori shouted, voice brimming with authority. My head lolled to the side, and black began to crowd my vision. I vaguely felt an oxygen mask being strapped to my face as my body was loaded onto a stretcher. Hands probed at my wound, gently extracting the knife from my side.

"She'll live," a voice said, and I turned my head, trying to find its source, but I couldn't move, couldn't feel my limbs. I was too far gone, tumbling down into a peaceful oblivion.

science fiction & fantasy

A Man-Made Heaven

Lydia Vlcek

Grade 11. Northwest High School, Grand Island, NE. Darbie Mazour, Educator. Honorable Mention.

There was not a star in sight on that smoggy night—and maybe it was better kept that way. At least, that's what she considered the first time she looked up. The second time, she decided it was perhaps better to have nothing to look up to at all. Bleak as this conclusion was, she accepted this truth and affirmed it as she continued on her elongated journey to what she considered to be a self-made torture.

As she found the will to walk against a once smooth, now tattered surface of gravelly concrete, a familiar sense of a dripping void continued to bog down on her emotions, and she couldn't help but let this null feeling almost draw her to a stop. But yet, she continued. There was no room to stop when dealing with a civilization. Both hands were swinging aimlessly at her side, incompetent for the job that lay ahead. Yet, she'd have to force them into a deranged sense of purpose if she were to continue without mistake.

All that lay in front of her was a verdureless, hilly and rock-filled valley with the only sign of inhabitants laying inside maliciously planned large structures. It was quite funny, really, considering the lengths those scientists had gone to preserve what was left of the dust from their wake. On this night in particular, they reflected an almost purple tinge against the rocks below, some areas almost projecting an orange-like glow from the patches of sand that lay below them.

The buildings did not make a sound—they just continued without failure to steal and then recycle any energy that dared to fall into their greedy radiance. It was the most efficient way humanity had discovered to thrive off of the new wasteland they'd created—the wasteland of the vast and unforgiving world of a man-made virtual reality. It was truly humanity's worst miracle.

Or at least, that's how she saw it. But in this world, nobody would hear. Nobody could hear. It was a feeling similar to being stuck in space—except, this fate was almost worst. All around her, there were people. Whether they were visible or an uncanny result of her imagination, she knew they were somewhere in the possible abyss. Just waiting. And as she finally advanced on the tallest building in sight, she let that same, sinking feeling drop down in its place in her heart.

This building didn't differ from the rest, as it still possessed those same gray tones that were the only affordable material at the time. The contents of those materials were of course plastic, similar to mostly all the man-made structures that dwelled here. With it being easy to make and even easier to scavenge from a time so long ago, it was an obvious choice. *How ironic that they now decide to live in their trash,* she considered, growing nearer and nearer to the beautifully destructive lilac glow the building emanated.

The glow itself was, of course, devoid of plastic. That would just simply be wasteful. Even though a good majority of the air here was nearly covered in plastic, the light itself was much more complex than that. The source of the beam was hidden somewhere deep within the compound of that gray building, and within that source of light, there was a small, yet efficient device that had the capability to seamlessly unite itself to small particles in the air. After it made that vital connection, from what she gathered, it ripped the particles to shreds, storing them for later. Sometime after that fiasco, through a process much too complex for her to understand, it was reverted into energy. How, she had no idea. However, she was one of the only ones left able to witness the result of the recycled energy.

Another thought tempted her away from reality the moment she was about to return. The thought in particular was the interesting desire that humanity had for making devices smaller, and then even smaller. The source of the stealing beam of light was nearly just as small as a simple grain of rice, perhaps even smaller.

She could remember now what would be the first and only time she was permitted to even have a glance at the small chip, and even now, she was still left in wonder and confusion as to why it was so essential to have such a complex chip so small. But, alas, she'd never come to a conclusion. She'd seen the chip on what was perhaps her third day here, and that was due to the fact that the person who came before her embodied what she defined as arrogance. The fool had coaxed her into sneaking to the energy source, to simply have a look at it. Considering that she hadn't seen them since that day, she let the thought pass back behind the wall of unnecessary memories.

Such an incompetent fool—they were set to fail here. Humanity allows no mistakes ... and as the daggering thoughts passed, she allowed herself one split second of sympathy. *Perhaps it's for the better th*—and before she could continue in her train of thought, a sudden pulse of vibrations began to ring at her feet. The vibrations moved in a sort of waving motion, nearly coming beneath her feet but then falling only a moment later. It was a very repetitive pulsing, and it never did seem to end. However, right as the panic began to grip her, she felt a sudden relief in realization. These waves were nothing but a beacon, a sort of warning to any animals that had somehow survived humanity's need for a stable food supply.

The vibrating defenses were almost always effective, and the only two times it failed were due to the small size of the animals in question. She'd never been there to witness the two intruders, but it was likely that either they were destroyed for energy preservation or, if they were lucky, the creatures were sent away to the lab for testing. If that were at all possible, they would at least get a few more minutes before oblivion.

Then again ... perhaps a quick end is best. In the lab, a quick death was never a guarantee. Whatever benefitted the lab in their mysterious experiments was never up for question. The reason being that there was no one to question them here. *What a bittersweet truth for humanity.* The thought constructed itself to aid her own guilty pleasure.

When she finally allowed her previous fears to come to a halt, she took a first step to where her undesirable job lay. The gray-toned buildings were now similar to that of a peakless mountain. Looking up and then down once again, she realized that the ground was truly the only thing to keep her stable against this vast mountain of a building. The plum glow of that deadly accurate beam was upon her now, and as she leveled out her head once again, she felt as though the hue was beginning to consume her. In a quick blink and a shake of her head, she took another step forward with the assistance of the quivering warnings following close behind. Of course, she at first felt the telltale signs that the purple hue had begun to seek out her energy.

Except, to its selfish dismay, there was none to take. And as she took another step once again, she felt the beacon's harassment no longer. How she completed this predetermined test was no secret to her. On the contrary, she knew nearly every aspect of exactly why she was allowed admittance to pass through the purple haze. Put shortly, it was simply because of her brain's own processes of passing information from one cell to another. As the machine targeted itself at one specific victim, it first took into account their own molecular construct. Considering that her brain was almost unrecognizable to the beam's actual target, she would always be granted a free pass. With the machine able to give any sort of CAT scan at any given moment of any known brain, it was almost impossible for it to fail. It had specifically learned to target any sort of scan that didn't fall into the category of a human's brain. All of this simplified within a few gaps of a second. No room for failure here, she reminded herself as she continued on.

Walking at an assured pace now, a more defined look began to detail the building in front of her now. There were cuts and small crevices that ran along one side, and against the other side ran a sustained banner that read "An Assured Beacon" in a bolded, black text.

The background of the said banner was, of course, transparent, as all things were now. Just a simple message conveyed upon a vastless and empty void to illustrate the lust for simplicity in a cloud of confusion. And sitting nearly perfectly in the center of the cursed gray building, there sat a bleached cover for a door. At some point, it was used, perhaps, to cover an entrance of a questionable area. Now, it was used for just about everything. No one could even catch a glimpse of the doors to buildings now, and perhaps it was better kept that way. To keep the eyes of the masses off of contentious areas meant less trouble for those who remained. However, this door differed from the rest. Being that it sat where the sun decided to shine nearly once a year, it got the most backlash for its existence. And so, it had faded into an obvious marker to display where the door really decided to hide.

An assured beacon, she thought to herself once again as she was now face to face with the sun-bleached gray surface. It was a simple trick, really, as all she had to do was walk through. To those outlookers, it would appear as if it were magic. However, all this classic trick needed was passive metals—a common material in current times. It was just simply metal that possessed a more extreme amount of electrons than protons. Simple, really, if you tried not to count for all the grueling years it took to make it safe to the public.

And once she took a step into the mystery, there was no turning back. The fading vibrations at her feet were now obsolete, and all that greeted her as she passed through was a dark mass of black with green peeking through the folds and a heavy thump against metal. Silence was all that really mattered now.

Inhaling, all that overwhelmed her nose was what remained of decay. It was a cruelly familiar smell that reminded her all too much of—well, human waste. Strange how specific the smell could be at the moment. Slowly lifting her head back to the highlight of the moment, she began to creep slowly forward once more. To her dismal amusement, the green began to dance upon the nearly water-like walls at her side. Taking a step would send them into a flurry of phony excitement until she took a single heartbeat to pause and look away. When such an event happened, they returned back into solid objects consisting of little to no value. Interesting as the lights at play were, she controlled her head perfectly still against the rush of emotions to the green object. And more than anything, ahead of her lay the source of the dancing lights. It was a blocky room that became more clarified as she grew ever closer. Being that it was in a constant state of changing to fit the eye of the beholder, she refrained herself from driving away her gaze.

As she grew closer, the previous sense of an undodgeable, nulling feeling attacked her heart once again. It was here, and it was here to stay as she could now almost feel the green being flashing against her face. The attack on her heart was a quick battle with a distinguished winner now taking complete reign on her emotions. She could no longer feel that fuzzy feeling that belonged to hope. It was a constant flow of tar that left sticky remains when it targeted one happy victim to the next. And now, as she came face to face with an arch that distinguished where all her trials began, she had to take a quick breath to keep from falling. To keep from becoming one with the floor below her. An exhale was all she needed to enter now. *There is no room for mistakes here,* was all she could consider as she took that last fatal step forward. And so, her fate was concealed in merry delight to the no one that watched.

Her fate itself, however, was anything but delight. And the first entry in her new path of life was met with a gruesome scene. In an instant of dismay, the scene was quickly brought to light—green light, specifically. Around her was a room dulled by its purpose, and with the walls containing nothing but a drabby gray and green rays peeking through the contained surface, it was almost as if it were doomed to an eternity of boredom. A few single lights also aided in the illumination of the room—however, considering their fittingly dull nature, they could barely even be considered as a dooming "beacon of hope." The phrase began to unsettle a moment without anger. However, she would not let herself succumb to any pathetic array of emotion since what her eyes traveled to next required her to proceed without an ounce of passion. And as her eyes fell upon the green light's creator, she felt that familiar tar of despair drop into her heart once again.

Her mind boggled her with answers to questions she already knew to distract her from a disgustingly accurate reality. *Those creatures that used to scurry through the caverns ... What were they—rats?* She nodded once more, a memory striking her mind at once. They were tiny things that used their last moments of life to try and find some source of food in this desolate wasteland—however, as the memory began to fade, she remembered that last bit of information that was crucial to end the story. Those rats had traveled much too close to the true terror of this reality, and now, as the memory faded from reality, she felt her legs moving helplessly forward to a destination her eyes became transfixed upon.

They were truly green—that was for sure. That glowing green slime appeared to almost move on its own terms, and she was sure they must have been ready to barge through at any moment. Preventing that terrible fortune was a thin, nearly invisible sheet of glass that was held together by a circular silver object. The silver was on its way to collecting a fine line of dust, which was unacceptable if she was to continue on her way.

However, her eyes could no longer ignore the object she had always dreaded. It was in front of her now—face to face, almost. Releasing a silent cry, she pulled her legs to a sudden halt. There was just dust that lay in front of her now, but she knew all too well that wasn't true.

Brushing off the dust carefully as though it would shatter, she revealed a painfully ghastly sight. At first, it would appear to an unknowing onlooker to be nothing but a mere mesh of slime. However, it was something truly much worse. A distorted face was the first thing that greeted her—however, distorted would be a kind understatement. The top of this mutated head was completely shaved, revealing a gaping hole that was without the necessary brain. The only clue remaining to tell you that this was at some point a human were the eyes that lay slightly below, and even those were far from anything humane. They were reddened from the time spent in this watery green prison, and slowly fading from their previous light thanks to the actual purpose of the green water. The rest of its body carried the same faded, greenish tinge that was unmistakably a token of the now modern society.

That green water's devious purpose was to preserve certain aspects of the human body that were deemed essential to the process of converting a mortal human into a digital age of virtual reality. It was a simple amount of chemicals, really, and it required only one person to look after it. Who though? Who was left to care for these deformed, useless bodies? The only one mortal left here—her.

And, within nearly a second of her blinking, many painfully familiar faces began to fly past her within an instant, all of them gone but yet so near. They all began to stare at her with that horrible, undead glare that never ceased, for it was their last instant of life. She let out an all too audible gasp that made their glaring fade away within an instant, and the only thing that was clear to her now was the contoured face that was lying in front of her. It became familiar to her once again, and the eyes were unmistakably recognizable to those of that insolent boy she had known far too close to the present day. He still remained arrogant, even in his supposed death, and as she took one step closer to the glass, she could utter only a simple murmur of apology before gasping once again. She allowed one single tear of weakness to escape from her eyes before taking a step back.

And with that, her mind turned null as she continued on to her cursed, mortal eternity of helping the dead into a man-made heaven.

Golden Hour

Ashley Binstock

Grade 12. Bishop Neumann Central High School, Wahoo, NE. Marisa Grady, Educator.

Portfolio Gold Key

flash fiction

Somewhere Before

The apartment steps sprawled before Cory, taunting her in the endless heat that stuck her strawberry pink hair in slick spindles to her neck. August had come with a vengeance, soaking Minneapolis in the kind of sun that ricochets off of windshields like laser beams and melts skin into butter. She had spent the past month soaking in its rays and swimming with Sam in any and every city pool that wasn't elbow to elbow with people. Cory watched a drop of sweat splatter on her not-so-white sneakers. The crystal bead was an unwanted reminder that the season would soon draw to a close.

"You ready?" Mr. Doberman asked, smiling. His salt-and-pepper hair held clinging strands of sweat as he positioned the table for them to lift up the cement staircase. Mr. Doberman, who had been their neighbor for years. Who had helped them maneuver their own furniture when they first moved into the building. Their neighbor who drove Cory places when her parents couldn't and who taught her how to paint a tree and then a cat and then her own mother. He had the kind of face that listened, the type of eyes that understood universes different from his own. It had only felt normal to help him move his new table up to his apartment. So when they brought it to the top of the empty staircase to rest, Cory didn't think anything of it. Didn't know what to do when his clammy hands closed around her waist. When she felt his hands slide over hers and lips press against her. *No*. Couldn't breathe, or move, or scream when suddenly he wasn't the same person anymore. And afterward, neither was she.

Somehow After

The world was a better place at sunset. Hazy tones of honey red dipped into the earth, drenching everything in a rose shade. Cicadas pitched into a crescendo of glorious praise at the heavenly wash and, suddenly, the earth began to turn again. But every sun eventually set against that limited horizon, and then night would come. Then the stifling heat of her family's two-bedroom apartment would swallow her alive. Cory's hands would dig tunnels through the sheets that swelled against her flesh in waves, sweat slipping down her cheeks in grimy drops. Words. Disgusting, haunting words would burn inside her ears until the flashing memories rumbled beneath the walls she'd buried them under.

Come on, don't you trust me?

I just want to have some fun.

It's not a big deal.

She didn't dream. She never dreamed about him or the way her blood had curdled against his touch. She tried not to think about how long he waited to do what he did to her that night. So why, then, did the skin beneath her eyes deepen into sable half-moons? Why did the girl in her mirror tremble with disgust as if in some distorted way, the fault was hers? The rusted bleachers stretched out before Cory, her bronze ring dancing from finger to finger when her friend's scrawny silhouette appeared from the corner of her eye, scattering the thoughts.

"You're late," Cory chided as Sam scrambled up the bleachers. The melting sun reflected in fractured rays that played across her dirty blonde hair like piano keys. She was wearing her usual pair of jeans that hung in tattered webs at the bottom. Reaching Cory, Sam tossed a bag of Doritos into her lap.

"Who brought the snacks again?"

Cory rolled her eyes, her forehead creasing in disappointment when she noticed the label. Realizing her mistake, Sam plucked the blue bag of Doritos from her hands and replaced it with her red one before crashing into a reclined position.

"So, what's up with the hair?" she asked.

A sudden crunch of chips sounded from Cory's palms as she made a conscious effort to relax her grip on the bag. She had dyed her hair again. A deep midnight blue that had managed to drown every pink ridiculous strand. It would have kept her awake at night, that taunting pink hair. It would have suffocated her with the smell of that stairwell and the lie of innocence. "Needed a change."

"I like it," Sam smiled. "It's like I'm friends with a Smurf."

Cory dipped her head until hair collected in front of her eyes in a cerulean veil. It was so stupid, sitting there with her friend and pretending to be normal. Listening to Sam call her a Smurf and aching, dying, to feel as human as she was. Fourteen was just a number she would see on street corners. Pink was a color that made her bend over toilet bowls. There had been something elemental in those hands that had erased parts of who she was. Somehow, some shift in the universe had distorted things. Somehow, being with her best friend in that moment was like breathing water. She wasn't made up of the same atoms anymore.

"Ya, I guess so." The sun seeped defiantly into the horizon and with it, Cory felt the forever goodbye of that golden hour.

flash fiction

I Pray the Lord My Soul Not Keep

Ashley Binstock

Grade 12. Bishop Neumann Central High School, Wahoo, NE. Marisa Grady, Educator.

Portfolio Gold Key

There was an ancient woman rooted in the upper left pew of the Church. She had aged like the oak—wooden, resilient, worn. Her marble knuckles pressed prayers against those hollow walls until the plaster blistered and curled against their merciless weight. She was ethereal. Entangled in those umber rows, unmoving in seraphic cement, inhuman in her faith.

People could not tear their eyes from her. As if she were a divine revelation, they peered over slouched shoulders and bobbing heads to steal glimpses of her frozen stature. They monitored the reverent dip of her snowy veil at unheard commands and, hypnotized, followed her into each rise. Each communion processional began with the priest stepping down from the altar to place the host in her reaching uncoiled hands. Even God seemed to understand she had become a part of that righteous earth.

Long after the final blessing had ended, she would remain burned into that farthest left pew. Priests came and went, all uttering in admiration the certainty of her spiritual gift. Parishioners' prayers fell in jealous clumps like the white hairs collecting along the woman's woven shawl. No one questioned how long she stayed there each night. No one had the power to vanquish her from her Father's house or question the intent of her fervent heart. Days and nights crumbled into years, and eventually no person could remember where the woman had come from, or at what time she would eventually creak away from the altar.

It was a stormy clandestine Tuesday, the day she died in that shadowed corner pew. With no living relatives to make arrangements, the women's church group, in solemn agreement, volunteered to organize the funeral. They visited her house that day. A compact, faded blue split-level home with a key hidden above the lamp post. Sliding the rusted metal into the lock, they heard a ceremonious click sound in the rain and loosen the hold on her door. It skidded open reluctantly, as if unfamiliar to the command.

A tangible smell of mildew and neglected litter boxes swelled from the push of air. Dust-coated light switches refused to stir when flipped. Upon opening the living room windows, the ladies' eyes widened in horror as they beheld the makeshift shrine. On the outstretching

flash fiction

length of wall, a monument had been constructed. Holy cards from every saint lay in conspiring circles, torn-out Bible pages with underlined words and blackened out paragraphs were scattered, and rosary beads rubbed down to skinny coffin-shaped pellets buried the floor.

An ebbing sensation of deep terror clung to the room on the sticky-tack stained walls and peculiar blemishes in the carpet. Finger smudges trailed her altar of questions that drawled an unending web across the space.

At what hour?

Signs in the sky?

What is in the Furnace?

Separation of the sheep?

Her bed left no imprint of usage, and the kitchen held no history of cooking stains. Every other part of the house was left undisturbed—besides that room. As if she had lived her life outside of the Church crawling to that gut-churning cage. The ladies found nothing they had come for that day. The old woman had kept no files, no birth certificate, nothing. The only possessions she had coveted lay in dissected mounds against that pale carpet floor. So, they left.

And no one talked about the way the priest had found her on that Tuesday. How he had arrived for adoration to discover her swollen grey corpse. No one spoke of the way she had slumped against the wooden pew behind her, as if she had been stretching, diving, away from the altar. Her face planted in the oak she'd begun to morph into, her eyes pressed roughly into the edge. And beneath her concave form, deep gouges written in the timber walls, her fingernails curved against claw marks.

Without You, Without Me

Ivy Block

Grade 11. Plattsmouth High School, Plattsmouth, NE. Christine Knust, Educator. Honorable Mention.

short story

Chapter 1. Early Love

Willow hated the water. In fact, she was terrified of it. Over and over she would avoid gatherings near the pool or the lake. Mr. Gervais was always kind to his daughter, suggesting perhaps she just stand by and think about joining in, or even just dip her toes in. Like she did with most things, Willow always prevailed; she got her way. She was not mischievous; she just always had a way to get herself on top. Mr. Gervais often ordered Willow around telling her to do chores, go to the lake, and other things she didn't wish to do. This would never work, not with Willow. Willow was a strange kid; she was eleven years old and had never said a word. She knew how to talk; she just chose not to. Mr Gervais thought she would never speak and would often take her to counseling. Willow hated counseling, and who could blame her? "It's not like daddy ever tries to understand why I don't talk. He just takes me to the doctors, and they say I'm stubborn."

short story

Willow was upset with her father, and her father was worried for her. He didn't understand why she wouldn't speak. She wasn't mentally challenged at all; in fact, she always had quite good grades, but with all his might she would not speak. Mr. Gervais was tired; it had been eleven years since she was born, and it was eleven years of specialists and experts saying the same old things that never seemed to work. One night they were eating dinner when Willow stood up. "Are you done, dear?" her father asked. Willow nodded. "Well, go get the fire ready while I finish up, will you?"

She smiled and walked off.

As Willow was feeding the fire, she heard a knock at the door. Mr. Gervais got up from the table to answer. "Another doctor?" Willow thought.

She was fed up with these people coming over and making her feel bad about the way she was. She turned to the fireplace as Mr. Gervais welcomed the man in. She was furious; she never expressed these feelings to her father, but she felt it was time to get her way. "Willow, won't you welcome Mr. P—"

Willow whirled around with a furious expression on her face. This expression quickly faded and turned into a red guilt. She looked down in shame. There was no doctor; it was Mr. Pilkington, their old neighbor. Mr. Pilkington leaned down and awkwardly patted her on the head. "Not one f'r greetin', m'self, 'til I know the person's werf the effort."

He smiled and walked off with Mr. Gervais.

This experience was painful for Willow. It upset her that she was so foolish. She should never get mad until she understands the situation well enough. She promised herself to keep her emotions in check; she hated hurting other people's feelings.

Three years earlier Willow and Lew were at the park swinging together when Lew asked Willow a question. "Willow," Lew hesitated uncomfortably, "what happens when you die?" Willow looked at her and cocked her head. "You know, like when people go away and never come back. What happens if we go away and never come back?"

Willow winced and curled up on the ground. "What's wrong, Willow?" Willow pointed behind them to a large fenced-in field. Lew picked her up, "Come on, I'll show you it's not that bad."

Lew was strong; Lew carried Willow a lot, and Willow felt comfortable in her arms. As they approached the gate Lew put Willow down and helped her stand. "What is this place?"

Willow started sobbing, and Lew comforted her. Willow latched onto Lew as they walked through the

short story

gate. Willow desperately wanted to go back, but Lew continued on through the light fog.

Lew stopped and sat Willow down. "See, come on, Willow. What is there to be afraid of?" Willow pointed to a large black stone. Lew walked over and examined it. "What do all these names mean?"

Willow started sobbing again. "Come on, Willow. What's going on? You're scaring me."

Willow pulled a small notebook out of her pocket and wrote frantically. She turned it so Lew could see. Lew smiled and hugged Willow. "There you go, sweetie. You did it. You wrote. I'm proud of you." Willow felt stupid; of course it was a trick. "And I'm sorry I brought you here. I know death scares you."

Willow felt betrayed, but she knew this was good for her, and she knew Lew would stay with her to keep her company. Willow wrote in the notebook again and showed Lew. "Of course we can."

Lew picked her up and carried her the rest of the way home. Willow felt safe.

The next day Willow and Lew were lying together in Willow's bed. Lew could tell Willow was upset with her. "I'm sorry, Willow; I just need you to know you're strong."

Willow looked down. "Please don't hate me, Willow."

Willow looked back up and brushed Lew's cheek. Lew felt bad; Willow was too forgiving. Someone could abuse that. Lew winced at the thought of that. Suddenly Mr. Gervais walked in. "Oh! ... Um ... Hello, Lew. When did you get here?"

"Last night. Sorry, I'll check in with you next time, Mr. Gervais. I'll be leaving now."

short story

And Willow was alone again, locked in her room from sun up to sun down.

Willow woke up breathing heavily; she was having a panic attack. She ran to her door; it was locked as always, so she pounded on it as hard as she could. A few seconds later she was in her father's arms crying. These were getting worse, and the more she was locked in her room the worse she felt. She was only in fifth grade, but her father insisted on her staying in there. "It's too dangerous for you to have access to sharp things outside your room, and it's unfair to ask us to get rid of them all," her father would say.

So she was stuck, in her room, for days on end, assisted breaks to the bathroom and watched thoroughly during meals. She went to school but had a nurse (hired by her father) to watch over her constantly to monitor conversations and stop any self harm, so she had no chance at making friends.

Everyone at her school hated Willow; they had no reason, though. They even admitted in private they didn't know why, they were just scared of her. Some nice kids tried to make friends with her sometimes, but they

short story

were warded off by the nurse, who hated listening to children's conversations. So Willow never spoke to the kids at school. She was alone. Completely alone.

Poems were a coping mechanism Willow used often to keep herself in control. In fact, on her wall she had painted her favorite that she had created:

In shadows of a perfect summit
Fostered pain grows ever stronger
Light was there, it seemed to plummet
Reaching pain as days grow longer
Pain is welcomed but pain is fierce
Where only perfect beings tread
Pain is quick and pain will pierce
As perfect beings lay their head
Needed only in those of light
Pain that perfect beings bare
That is welcomed without fright
For only those who truly care

This poem was a tribute and a wish, a tribute to her life and a wish for her death. She had written it when she was seven years old. It was comforting to Willow to think of her own death. "Surely if it happens to everyone why should I fear my own?"

She hated thinking about others' deaths, though. The thought often came when she thought of her own, so she generally avoided the subject.

It was late August 2011 when Willow first met Lew; they were friends throughout elementary school, but they never spoke because of Mrs. Merchant (her nurse). Lew had a way with Willow that no other kids understood. By just looking at each other, they could have a whole conversation. In Willow's first year of middle school, she received a bike from her father. Though she had no intention of riding it, she showed much appreciation toward her father. She knew what this bike meant; it meant freedom. It meant Willow was responsible enough to go outside alone. And she did. She took that bike along streams and through the woods. She would listen to the forest for hours.

That year, in early October Mrs. Merchant died. Willow's father couldn't find anyone else to be her nurse, and when he explained the situation to his daughter, he saw a glimmer of hope in her eyes.

He had to let her go.

He had to let her live more freely.

So Mr. Gervais did not hire a new caretaker. She was free, more than she could have ever imagined. She rushed into class the next morning and found herself the center of attention. Willow did not like the children's questions, nor their volume. She was surrounded by the children and had nowhere to go. So she fell down and cried. She cried until they left her alone. This became a pattern: when new kids spoke to her, she broke down.

short story

Until it was like before, no one to talk to. No one who liked her. Except Lew. Lew was there from the start; it was she who told the other kids to leave her alone, and now it was she who made sure Willow would never be alone.

Early the next summer, Lew and Willow went on a walk together. It became a usual thing; they would go along the streams and through the forest together. Willow liked this more; she didn't feel lonely in the woods anymore. When the birds chirped, they chirped with joy. When the wind blew, it was gentle and calming. She loved Lew with all her heart; she was everything Willow ever wanted.

Willow and Lew were walking together one late summer night. The stars were so bright, the wind was soft, and the forest was magical. As they reached an opening, Willow stopped. There were hundreds of fireflies lighting up the shadowing tree canopy. A small creek flowed next to them, reflecting the stars into their eyes. It was a perfect moment. Willow was gazing up at the fireflies. Then as she looked down, Lew was closely looking at her. Willow stared into her eyes as she walked closer. She wished in that moment that Lew would make love to her in that forest. Lew kissed her passionately. "We're too young for that, dear. For now let's settle for girlfriends."

Willow went home and fell into her bed; she couldn't sleep. All night she thought of that moment.

She colored pictures and wrote the story down; she did everything to capture that moment forever. It wasn't enough. She wasn't enough. What if Lew left her? How did she know what Willow was thinking? She fell asleep, heart racing; she had nightmares of Lew leaving her forever. She was love sick.

Chapter 2. Voices of Pain

Willow was conflicted. She wanted to scream to the world that she kissed Lew, and that the two of them were dating. At the same time she knew her father wouldn't be happy with her being in a relationship so young. She decided to keep it quiet but she wasn't happy about it. Willow and Lew looked at each other differently from that day on. In the classroom Willow would notice Lew staring at her with the most beautiful smile. And Lew noticed Willow's precious eyes saying, "I love you, Lew. I just wish I could tell you out loud." They were distracted so often both saw it reflected in their grades.

The two girls were at each other's houses more often than their own. One night while they were in bed together, Willow was pleasuring Lew when Lew's Mother walked in and screamed in shock. "Get out! Get out! Get the hell out!" Willow was ashamed. She stood up and bolted out the door. Lew was tired of this; she opened her mouth to scream back at her mother.

short story

No words came out, she heard a voice whisper, *No one can hear you.*

"Where is that voice coming from?" Lew thought

It doesn't matter, you're never going to be good enough for her.

"What the hell is going on?" Lew thought. "Am I going insane?"

You already are insane.

"Who the hell are you? Get out of my head!"

At that moment she came back to; her mother was furious. "What do you have to say for yourself?"

Lew started shaking in fear. She wept to her mother to forgive her. She did not mention the voices.

As Lew described the voices to Willow, Lew noticed the fear in Willow's eyes. She stopped. "What's wrong?"

Willow wrote down on her pad and handed it to Lew. "I've heard them, too." Lew was shocked. "How long have you heard them?"

Lew knew the answer. "Why did you never tell me?"

Willow looked down. "Hey," Lew said. "Don't feel bad. I'm just trying to understand."

The two girls were desperate to know what these voices were, but with only each other they knew nothing. The next few months were horrible. Lew started hearing voices constantly, and Willow worried for Lew's health. She had noticed cuts appearing on Lew's arms, hands, wrists, thighs, waist and stomach. Willow wanted to help, but she had no idea what to do.

Chapter 3. Red Signs

They were only teenagers; they didn't know better. Willow and Lew made love every day they saw each other. It was all they could do to drive the voices away. They hated it. At this point love was just another failed way to fix a bad problem. Lew was in shambles: she had nothing left to hold on to, her mother hated her, her father had died, and Willow was terrified of her. She had nothing left to live for.

Willow was in the woods alone one day. It was beautiful out; she had gone out with her bike to get to Lew's house. She was following a small stream when she saw something strange, like a small red fish swimming by in the stream of clear water. Another swam by. A few more. Soon the stream was bright red. She quickly rushed up the hill to see the source of the stream. It was a sewer grate that ran straight to Lew's house. Willow ran up the hill and rode her bike for the very first time, straight to Lew's house. She rushed in the door and pushed Lew's mother aside. She ran for the bathroom. She was right. Lew was gone.

There were four sounds Willow heard in the next few minutes. The first was the shriek of Lew's mother piercing through Willow's thoughts, paralyzing Willow

short story

and causing the second sound. This sound was the high-pitched ring of shock and the numbness of thought that Willow felt as she dropped to the ground in grief. The third sound minutes later was that of an ambulance, the looping siren ringing constantly as they rode to the hospital. And the last was that of a heart monitor, the final sign that Willow was again alone.

The Game of Your Fears

Anastasia Brock-Ondresky

Grade 10. Boys Town High School, Boys Town, NE. Beth Sulley, Educator. Honorable Mention.

short story

Running was the only thing I knew and the only thing I could do to stay alive. Last December at 2:05 AM it all started: the killing, the fighting, the shootings, and everything to make my life a misery. I can still remember the sound of the sirens going off and the announcement for all to be free and live how they wanted. For some reason, I think I was the only one that was not aware of what was going to happen next. All I can think of from this agony is death. The only way to stay alive is to take people's lives and care into consideration.

I found a group of three hiding in the closet of an abandoned house with no guns and no way to protect themselves. I decided to take them under my wing and show them how to stay alive. Alez, oldest and smartest out of all, told us that we needed to find ways to protect ourselves if we ran out of ammo and weapons. Mia, the youngest, was very traumatized to see her own mother die in front of her eyes. She hasn't talked since; all she does is walk where we walk and show up to all the things we show up to. Snow, the middle child and the bossiest, asked what was to happen next. Honestly to me this

short story

all was a nightmare. I grew up where we went to school every day, celebrated holidays, and didn't try to kill each other over the last loaf of bread. Things have changed, and I have changed too. I had to find a way to stop all this madness, but sometimes it was hard to figure out a way. I would have to change not only my mind but others' in the world right now.

I decided for the group that we needed to go to a more secure place. I remember an old cellar that my great-grandma used to have. It was full of food and supplies that could be useful for us. We were leaving at 4:00 AM, before anyone woke and decided to kill. I was up first for night watch, and I hoped nothing would happen to me. I was not just afraid for myself but for all that were with me. It was really hard to stay awake after the day of traveling every which way to find myself a home. I drifted off into sleep and woke to the sound of a wolf howling, knowing that I needed to wake everyone and start traveling. It was a very eerie and quiet morning to take these people out in the world. I told myself that all I need to do is to stay alive for 2 miles and everything would be fine.

Mia looked exhausted, and she could barely walk. I put her on my back and let her go to sleep. I walked at a slow, diligent pace. I was hopeful to not be in an outbreak of violence. But that dream never could come true. I walked on the road of my great-grandma's drive, relieved that the sun was coming slowly over the horizon. In the past this was no scary place, but now in the present it was scary. I needed to run to get there on time before anyone took their posts inside of their yard. I had barely thought that when I saw this man that was derelict and frail. It was to my surprise that he greeted me with a comforting smile, then raised his gun and cocked as he was about to shoot. I turned around with Mia on my back and tried to put her on the ground so I could fight to protect these children. He lowered his gun. "Sorry, ma'am, I did not know that there was a child involved. I will let you go now."

I finally found one person that had some common courtesy to children. I bumped Mia higher on my back. I speed walked onto Grandma Anne's porch, but the door was locked, of course. I knew she always kept a spare key inside the leprechaun in the flower bed near the stairs. I walked over and picked up the frozen statue and grabbed the key inside. I walked back up to the door, stuck the key in, and hoped it would unlock. It was difficult, but it did unlock to the forceful grip of my hands.

I walked inside the house still frozen in time. Of course there were no lights, but the sunlight was good enough until I got into the cellar below the basement. I had only one flashlight, so it was a little difficult to guide the four of us down the stairs. I imagined when

short story

I was a little girl and I ran throughout this basement of mysteries to find something new to play with. I needed to focus on now and not the easier years. I walked into the pantry to find a note from my grandma.

> Dearest Granddaughter,
> I knew that you would come here. I have stocked up the cellar full of supplies and food for you. The only thing I can do now is run. If this ever ends, I will first look here as I know you will be here.
>
> Stay safe and stay alive,
> Grandma Anne

I let one single teardrop hit the ground. When I heard a gunshot, I told everyone to stay there as I had forgotten to lock all the doors. I thought that this would never end. I tried so hard with the life I had before to not let little things affect me. I went up to the creeping stairs and locked *all* doors, windows, and vents, and made sure that it looked as if no one had entered. I went back down and locked the basement doors, as now this was our home.

As I walked back into the dark and chilling pantry, I noticed the three standing there with complete terror on their faces. I stated, "We are safe for now. The only thing that we can do now is stay alive." I paused and remembered that there was a water source down here; that meant bathing and hydration. I needed to set ground rules before we all could finally feel safe.

"I will have a few rules and that is all. Number 1, no drinking or eating anything if you have already had a meal without permission. Number 2, do not, I repeat, do not go up these stairs for any reason."

Everyone including Mia shook their head in agreement. We all settled into what I guessed would be our forever home. Everyone looked exhausted including me. I needed to set up before anything. Lulu, Mia's stuffed bunny, hit the floor. She scrambled to pick it up and I said, "Mia, you can go and play over there; there should be an oil lamp. Click it twice and you should be good." She shook her head in agreement.

"Alez and Snow, I need to talk to you."

We walked over into the corner where the dusty washer and dryer still remained and I told them, "We need to fix this problem of life and death before it becomes normal. I need to remember that you guys are just kids, but we need to do all that we can to change it." Alez thought for a moment and then blurted out, "If we go to the main building of control, we can flip the switch and change laws back to normal. I read it in a manual of the old house I was in."

It took me a minute to process. "Can you repeat what you said slower so I can understand?"

short story

Snow butted in. "He pretty much said that there is a main switch in the control room of the city and we can turn it off but it will be a long journey. Blah! Blah, Blah."

Okay, I thought to myself, even if I could get to this control room, how would I keep these kids safe. Hmm ... is all that I was thinking. "Okay, well, I need to go alone. I will leave the day after tomorrow, an hour after sun down. I have a lot of planning to do. I need you two to stay here and look after Mia, please. It will be a gruesome journey for me. I just need for you guys to be safe. Does that sound alright?"

Alez had a solemn look on his face, and it looked like he was about to break down crying. He looked up and asked, "How will we know that you have survived?"

"Well," I said, "honestly there is only one way and that's *the announcement*. If you don't hear it in 24 hours, you will know I have not made it and that you now must stay here, right here, until someone can do the job I was trying to do."

"Well," he acknowledged, "I guess that works."

"I have a lot of prepping that I can do before I take a hike to the control room. I need you to occupy Mia as I will not be telling her that I am leaving. I need to do this so she doesn't try to make me stay one way or another." Snow and Alez shook their head in agreement.

I started the prepping work. I needed to make sure that these people knew how to use these items in this place. I need to teach them how to regulate food consumed and how to output it in a polite manner. I had so much to do in so little time. I gave Mia my old toy box with toys that I once played with, to make sure that she was not a bother to anyone. I made sure that everyone had their own space to sleep and to eat. It was very difficult to get Snow to stop complaining about having to eat off the same fork as everyone else but honestly we have to do what we have to do in moments of crisis. We always took turns eating as we only had one plate and one cup. I always tried to make sure I had enough food for everyone to have seconds, but sometimes it did not work out that way. I needed to set a limit on food before it ran out. I made a plan and explained it to both Snow and Alez and let them know that all they had for right now is hope that everything would be okay.

As planned, I left two days after the idea was brought to my attention. I slowly walked up the creaking stairs, trying not to wake anyone. I unlocked the door and started the walking I knew I was going to have to do. So, I got told by Alez that the control building was 19 miles from here. It was going to be a long journey, and I knew I needed to get there before anyone woke. That meant I had 5 hours of a dark and long journey ahead of me. It was dark and I was scared. I knew that all I could do was to push myself to do better. I arrived at the city limits ahead of schedule, so I was very hopeful that I could get

short story

to the control building before daybreak. I climbed hills that stretched into farms of mournful fields that once grew corn.

I finally reached the road that led me right into the control room. I walked slowly, as I knew in my gut that something was going to happen. To my surprise, I reached the building with no problem. It looked as if there were bricks and guns stacked up along the building and there was no one to be seen. I tried to nudge the doors and they were locked. There was a window that was ground level. I knew I could climb in, and I did just that. I realized there were no weapons, no anything in the room. I walked in. Somehow something knew I was doing something for the good, because I did not have to figure out anything. I pulled the lever that was described to me. All of a sudden, the room lit up with joyful energy and hopefulness. I heard an announcement that all have survived the test.

I woke into brief happiness, but to my surprise I was sitting in a chair with wires and cords surrounding me. I was honestly scared. I was unaware of what was going on, and I then realized this was all a test. It was a test of survival and a test of caring. I thought for all this time it was real.

A woman walked in and said, "Welcome back. I am excited to have you back." I looked at her in confusion. "Oh! You are the ones that we put into the program without you knowing. There were four of you: Mia, Snow, Alez, and of course you. Honestly I just need to congratulate you for surviving The Game of Your Fears. Now this is a fear only you have, so no one in this building knows that you had the dream."

I looked at her. "The others," I stated, "they were there as well."

"I see ... the dream you had was very different from the ones that they had. I need to assure you that all people are safe, and you are free to go whenever you like."

I sat there in disbelief until I saw the sun shining and cars driving down the road. I finally knew I was safe and had nothing to worry about.

short story

Platonic Soulmates

Charlotte Coughlin

Grade 9. Bishop Neumann Central High School, Wahoo, NE. Marisa Grady, Educator. Gold Key.

short story

"You're going to fall," I told her.

"I know," she said.

My best friend was one of those people that made you feel good. She was free, and being around her felt like dancing even though it looked bad or singing and not caring how it sounded. She was a free being, a fae incarnate, or an old deity of the world come back to check on humanity. She bled kindness and gushed fire. She was a sun-kissed human with the stars on her skin and the earth in her veins. Her eyes were always searching for something. When they found whatever it was they were looking for, her hands would go still. She would stop, as though she were caught in headlights. Time stopped. I stopped.

"If you know, why are you still leaning so far?" I asked her. "If you fall, I'm not catching you."

She huffed and leaned back, propping herself on her hands. "Sorry, mom, my bad," she drawled.

I gave her the stink eye and went back to watching the sunset. It was incredible. The hues seeped into the clouds and dyed them all the shades of a blotchy blush.

The sun had already dipped below the horizon, and as the colors faded into bruised purples and blues, I looked at her. She took my breath away every time.

She was still. Her eyes had found the sunset, and when I looked into them, I was reminded for probably the millionth time of how fitting her name was: Hazel. Her eyes were fifty shades of beautiful, and whenever we locked gazes, I was reminded of forest floors and the little white mushrooms that grew on dead trees.

Her silhouette was glowing against the last straggling rays of sunlight, painting her chocolate skin in honey. As the day finally faded, she turned to me.

"We should go," she said, dusting off her hands. "We have school tomorrow."

She got up and brushed her hands off one more time before offering me a hand to get up. I took it, and she pulled me to my feet. I was taller than her.

"Okay," I sighed. My breath made the little flyaway hairs on her head shiver. "We should head back before it gets too dark."

Hazel bobbed her head in agreement and turned away. I followed her, our shadows casting long, disproportionate reflections of us on the concrete. As we walked away from our hangout and back to the tiny town we called home, we talked. We always talked. Some people think that when you know someone well enough, you don't have to say anything, and maybe

short story

that's true. But for me and Hazel, we said it anyway. We talked about how she saw a dead bird that morning and how I had spilled my cereal yesterday. We talked about all the colors in the sunset and the new songs we heard.

It was natural, the way we conversed. I could have known her all my life, the way we spoke. But she moved here only last year. Yet I felt like I'd known her for eons.

My house was closest to the edge of town, and as we entered our suburban prison once again, the only light left in the sky was so faint that you could start to see the stars. Hazel's house was another four blocks away. I turned to her.

"Do you want to just stay at my place tonight?" I asked. "It's already dark out. You'd probably trip over a rock or something and break your neck if you tried to walk home now."

Hazel snorted and started walking down the tiny driveway to my front door, her puffy brown hair bouncing in its bun. "You ask me to stay like you think I wasn't already planning to. Your dad bought ice cream today, didn't he? I'm not passing that up."

I smiled and followed her, shaking my head. "I knew I shouldn't have told you we bought cookie dough."

My home was Hazel's home. It was a "mi casa es su casa" vibe. Hazel stole one of my hoodies to sleep in and I dished up the ice cream. She turned on *Top Gun* again. It was her favorite movie. We sprawled on my bed and ate ice cream while Hazel quoted every other scene in the movie. After so long, we fell asleep. I lay on her stomach and snored while she drooled on my favorite pillow.

I'm not ashamed to say I loved Hazel. She was my favorite person. She always made me feel wanted. I hadn't always felt wanted. She was a pure person, the kind that God makes when he's in a good mood.

But she had always leaned too far over the edge. She had always been like that. She was reckless and unshackled. And sad, apparently.

Hazel never told me how much she was hurting. When you really know someone, you're not supposed to have to say anything. You just know. But me and Hazel told each other everything. I thought we told each other everything. She didn't tell me everything.

I loved my best friend. But I never told her, and then I lost her.

I still remember the day she left. The day that I began to hate things that reminded me of her. The day when the taste of cookie dough ice cream began to make me feel sick and the day that I stopped looking at sunsets and the day I threw the disc with *Top Gun* on it out.

I was out for a walk. I just wanted to see the sunset, maybe take a picture. I had wandered to our bridge. It had always been the best spot for taking pictures of the horizon. It was the only place without houses or trees blocking the view of the horizon. The river below gaped so deep that nothing grew tall enough to block the skyline. It was a walking bridge over a man-made, long abandoned canal.

Hazel was there.

She was sitting on the edge again, in her usual spot. Her shirt rippled in the wind, and as I watched, she leaned over the railing.

I noticed her shoes on the pavement, set in a neat pair.

She stepped over the railing and onto the ledge on the other side. She untied her hair. It curled in the breeze and the light from the sunset outlined each strand in gold. She looked candied in the sweet light. The rays of luminescent light caressed her in a warm, nonexistent hug.

She turned around and grasped the railing with both hands, her back toward the pit. The paint flaked off where her palms squeezed the decrepit old bars. Her bare feet pattered softly against the tiny strip of worn concrete.

With her face toward me, she finally spotted me standing at the entrance to the bridge coming from town. We locked gazes; forest floors and mushrooms. She looked shocked for a moment before she smiled. If not for the fading sunlight shining on her face, I might never have seen the tear roll down her cheek, golden in the half-light.

"You're going to fall," I told her.

She looked at me like I was a small child that didn't quite grasp the situation. And maybe I didn't. Maybe I was being selfish, loving her enough to want her to stay. All I wanted was to watch *Top Gun* together and go on walks and Face Time each other in college and send each other ridiculous cards on our birthdays.

She was my best friend, and I loved her the way you love something like your sight; you always have it with you, and you need it, and when you lose it, you're not quite sure what to do. You have to learn a whole new way of living without it. You don't realize how much you need it until you're in danger of losing it.

And I lost it.

"You're going to fall," I told her.

"I know," she said.

Dreams Are Just Dreams, Aren't They?

short story

Aryanna Petty

Grade 10. Boys Town High School, Boys Town, NE. Beth Sulley, Educator. Silver Key.

I'm running down the hall, gasping for breath as I hear the footsteps behind me. The flickering lights above me are blurring my vision as I risk a single glance over my right shoulder. I turn a sharp corner and hear a snap as my heel breaks. I fall face first on the clammy linoleum. Whimpering, I pull both of my shoes off as fast as possible. As I clamber up onto my knees to start running, I feel something strike the back of my head. The last thing I see before falling is the dark nothingness of the hallway.

I jolt awake, my sheets sticking to my back with sweat. I look around frantically, my breathing slowing as I take in the familiar pale green of my walls. I let myself fall back onto my pillow, my mouth dry with fear as I recall the events of my dream. It's been the same dream for the past few months, the ending never changing. But dreams are just dreams, right?

My thinking gets interrupted by the shrill beep of my alarm clock. I groan, turning it off and sliding out of bed. I stand in front of my mirror, grimacing at my pale blond hair that looks impossible to brush. My thoughts are quickly interrupted by my phone ringing. I run over, answering it.

short story

"Hello?" I ask, tucking the phone under my chin while I look for my jeans. My best friend's singsong voice floats from the phone.

"Hey, so like I know you're really busy with your sister and stuff, but I really need my decorating goddess to come help me get the gym decorated for the fundraiser tonight."

I laugh to myself. I can always count on Amari, the queen of last-minute phone calls, to save me from certain death by babysitting. "I should be able to make that work, lemme just talk to my parental units and get back to you."

"*Thank you,* just make sure to tell them that the gym has to be *completely* decorated by 5:15, and that I only have like six other people."

"Message received. I'll text you later, alright?" I say, finally finding my jeans at the bottom of my closet and pulling them on in a very clumsy, one-handed manner.

"Sounds good! Thalia, you're an angel and I would love to stay and chat but I gotta go. My brothers are trying to steal the rest of my frozen waffles. *Daveon, I swear if you touch one more I'm gonna s—*"

I hung up before I heard the threats that always came when Amari's dealing with her younger brothers.

short story

I threw my hair up in a careless ponytail before grabbing my bag and running out the door.

Standing in the gymnasium after three straight hours of decorating, I can't help but feel a burst of pride in my chest.

"It looks like I just walked into a Barbie Mermadia funhouse," announced Amari as she flounced over. Thalia's best friend was on the shorter side, but she always made up for it with her shoes, giving her a few extra inches in height. Her hair was black and curly, reaching to her mid-back. She had eyes that were every green hue of the forest in summertime, framed with eyelashes that gave her the look of childhood innocence, though it didn't quite match the mischievousness of her smile.

I shrug. "I tried, and I mean it looks good," I say, slumping down into a nearby chair and sliding my shoes off. "The actual dance is at what time?" I ask, looking up at Amari.

"6, 6:15-ish," she said with a smile as she checked the time. "Speaking of which, you're getting ready at my place, so we better get going."

Amari's room looked as if she had tried to fit every single thing she found interesting into a livable space. The main points of focus were her bed, vanity, and dresser, all covered in sketch pads, makeup, clothes, dishes, and the like. Three out of her four walls were a blazing orange,

short story

all hand-painted. One wall of which had a silver, floor-length mirror propped up against it, scarves and necklaces hanging off the corners. The last wall was the one behind her bed, it was plastered top-to-bottom with an ever-changing set of posters, all displaying her current interest in shows, movies, bands, and hobbies.

I look up as Amari stands up from ransacking her closet long enough to fling a dress at me. I pick it up, staring at the soft pink material.

"It's long enough, isn't it?" Amari asks, migrating toward her dresser. "Check my jewelry drawer for my teal and gold set. I'm trying to find heels that I thought would look super cute," she says, rifling through her drawers.

I sigh softly, "You know I don't wear heels, Amari."

She looks up. "I know, I know, but like it's a *dance*. And you can't wear a dress like that with *Converse*." Saying the last part of her sentence in such a way, I began to think I had committed some sort of crime. And in all honesty, I probably did in the eyes of fashion law. "Now get ready!" she exclaimed playfully.

"Fine, fine," I began ruefully. "But just this once," I added quickly. I toss the dress over my shoulder and start searching for the jewelry.

Walking into the gymnasium I clearly remember why I don't wear heels. I inhale sharply, cursing my general clumsiness. I nod to a few kids from class as I walk through the sea of people. I notice my friends sitting

short story

at a table, relieved to have them here. Amari and our friend Jayden are currently in an argument about something stupid when I sit down, neither of them noticing me. I sit next to Reina, a fiery redhead who enjoys watching our two friends go back and forth more than she should.

"So what's this one about?" I ask, gesturing toward the other side of the table.

"If I remember correctly, vampires and werewolves," she says matter of factly. "Jayden is for vampires. Amari is for werewolves." Her voice dropped a little. "Personally Amari's argument is more convincing."

I nod. "Interesting, but did anyone have the idea to bring in the topic of 'Thalia-is-wearing-heels-and-feels-like-her-feet-are-trying-to-fall-off'?"

Jayden finally looked up. "Wait, repeat that ... did I just hear the words 'wearing,' 'heels,' and 'Thalia' in the same sentence?"

I rolled my eyes. "Yea, something like that. I hope you heard me say, '*My feet are trying to fall off.*'"

Amari beamed. "Hey, so I would love to take as much credit for this as I can, but I'm getting texts to refill the punch." She gave a quick wave before flouncing away.

Reina shakes her head after her. "Have any of you guys found an off button? That girl needs a charge."

"Honestly I think the only thing that could stop Amari is death," I say with a laugh.

short story

Jayden shrugs. "She's a lot more productive than all of us, though. Have you seen the things she can do with a two-by-four, a can of spray paint, and a lighter? Also how does she only run on a single cup of coffee? It's ins—"

Jayden's remark was cut off suddenly by the uniform rumble of the lights shutting off, followed by the panicked shouts of those around us. Before I could say anything, I heard the loud shriek of metal-on-metal, drowning out the screams. But as fast as it had started it stopped.

"What just happened?" I ask, trying to keep my voice steady.

"I don't know, but I don't think it could've been anything good ..." Reina says softly.

I reach for my phone, my panic rising when I can't feel it in the dark. This all feels too familiar. I pause as the lights turn back on, my heart jumping out of my chest. I look up, trying to bite back the sudden wave of déjà vu, hoping it isn't true, hoping the screams are for something else.

My eyes see her way before my brain can acknowledge who she is. Amari. Hanging from the rafters by a cable. Her body slack and lifeless above the stage. Her bare feet are about a few inches off the ground. Her throat and wrists are slashed, the blood running down her body in thick crimson rivulets. It looks like some

short story

sort of sick reenactment of a puppet, as if she's going to come to life, dancing across the stage with her usual animated fervor. But I know she won't. I hear Jayden and Reina gasp behind me, but I don't flinch as I hear them start yelling her name, because it won't matter, none of us are making it out of here. I look at the spray-painted backdrop behind Amari's swaying body, knowing the thick, black lines that form the scrawling words from my nightmares before I even read them.

"Dreams are just dreams, aren't they?"

FLYING

ANNA ROGERS

Grade 8. Hastings Middle School, Hastings, NE. Stephena Gilmore, Educator. Silver Key.

short story

She thought her mom was on the verge of kicking her out. Cassandra's mom screamed and yelled, purple sparks flying off of her and dissipating in the air. "You have been out with that *rascal* of a girl all night!" She came three inches from her face, her tomato-red face seething with rage. "You listen to me, Cassandra Moskovitch. We were born witches for a reason! We plague young women with horrid spells as a *career path!*" During her rant, a book came flying off the shelf and hit her in the head. "If I see you with that human girl *one* more time, I'll—*ow!* Oh, this damn volume!" She grabbed hold of the book fluttering over her head and threw it with accuracy, right into its position before. She turned as if she was going to say something but stormed into the other room instead.

Cassandra squatted in her position and cried. Kiki, the resident black cat, came to comfort the girl. She pushed her head into Cassandra's wet hands, easing her despair. *Maybe she would finally learn what to do with her life, and move out,* she thought. Maybe the daughter of the famed Sylvia Moskovitch would finally move out.

short story

She scooped up Kiki into her arms. Her legs were sore from her position on the floor. If Cassandra did leave, she would kidnap the cat on the way out. Cassandra's mother yelled at her often. *You're making those pitiful potions again?! Learn some real witchcraft, girl!*

"The girl" actually just wanted someone to relate to. She had three brothers and the only female she had ever known was her mother. She'd never felt resentful toward human females—but more curious. She had met that girl on the street. Alanah. Maybe if her mother wasn't so invasive she could actually have a social life. Cassandra cradled the cat and strode to her bedroom. Vines hung from every corner of the ceiling, making a mess of greenery. But it also made a natural canopy over Cassandra's resting space, which she found rather innovative. On one side of the room, there was a large, thick iron cauldron. The neighboring wall had shelves and shelves of ingredients. Centipede exoskeletons, oddly colored mushrooms, a variety of dried flowers, animals, and other things. Kiki lept from the young woman's arms to rest on a soft pillow.

Cassandra sat on the stool by her cauldron. She had cast spells on her mother before, to try and make her understand why she felt so lonely. But each time was an undeniable failure.

Eventually, she gave up. *Maybe a magic circle would work?* she thought. As if on cue, her mother barged through the door. Cassandra had informed her mother about knocking but it seemed she didn't understand the concept. The older woman was less red now and swathed in a brown cloak. "Come, girl. Get ready. We're going somewhere." Being the dutiful child that she was, she obliged and threw on her emerald-green cloak.

Another thing that fascinated Cassandra: flying. The women both mounted their brooms and took flight. They both ascended, the ground beneath them becoming smaller and smaller. It was a clear night and you could clearly see stars and the visible planets. The moon shone a gorgeous white light over the landscape. Cassandra was sure they were going to the mushroom forest to gather ingredients for another brutal spell to cast on an innocent young girl.

But they didn't land. They sped right over the group of trees that made the forest. They now flew over a vast lake, the moonlight casting a reflection of the sky. "I understand, you know. The loneliness." Cassandra didn't like that word. "Understand." People said it often to her to play with her emotions. Cassandra noticed that her brother used the word "understand" a lot. He had never helped her by saying it though. Her mother spoke once more. "I had a friend. Hayden. She wasn't a witch." Cassandra now took interest. "She was probably my best friend. Or, if I was being accurate, my only friend." The daughter looked confused. "But don't you go to coven meetings with your witch friends all the time?"

"They aren't really my friends. Just useful colleagues I happen to be acquainted with." Cassandra could tell she was going somewhere with this so she held back her questions. "Hayden went to school with normal people ... normal girls. She invited me to a picnic in mid-spring, to watch the cherry blossoms. But when I got there, dressed up with my hat and broom, the girls seemed to be having an intense conversation. The girls were telling Hayden that I shouldn't be trusted. That I was dangerous. That people like me made the world a bad place to live in. And she believed. My only friend said that the world would be better without me.... I was angry. I turned the two girls into rings. And Hayden ..." Cassandra was horrified as she glanced at her mother's rings. Silver, gold ... and ivory.

"Girls are vile," her mother said. "Immature. They're only interested in seducing boys with their looks."

"I understand that you are angry. But you are also afraid. Afraid to find different people to bond with. Afraid to find human ladies that are good and mature. You might not be interested in trying, and I'm not going to try and change your mind. Mom, I'm a woman now. I'm over 19 years old. I'm leaving tomorrow morning to live my own life."

The older woman gripped Cassandra's arm. "You will *not* receive help from me." Cassandra pulled off her mother's hand and smiled. "I don't need it." She turned her broom and made the flight back to her room. She felt afraid and sad—like she had just made a terrible mistake. But she also felt proud. She would be able to live her own life now. Cassandra would leave the next morning. Maybe she could find her friend again.

short story

We're More Than That

Victoria Bogatz

Grade 8. Lewis & Clark Middle School, Bellevue, NE. Michelle Kastl, Educator. Silver Key.

novel writing

Chapter 4. Nyeshi

"I'm going to miss you, Moriah," I say to Moriah's reflection as I smooth my hair in the mirror. Turning around, I embrace her. This hug is a goodbye to our friendship. It's the last time she'll help me get ready. It's the last time I'll ever see her again.

I don't keep in contact with my servants—it's not allowed. I just have to say goodbye.

I hear her sniffle near my ear, and I'm on the verge of tears, too. It's like déjà vu, the same thing year after year, never getting any easier.

When we pull apart, Moriah wipes her eyes with a handkerchief.

"I should go greet the new servants," I say. "Thank you. You've been amazing."

Moriah smiles. "It's been an honor serving."

I give a small smile, not wanting to say anything else. Then, I head to where my new maid and butler will be waiting.

My butler's name is Caleb Abrams. He's from Ames, one of the largest and poorest sectors in Cypress. Short brown hair, hazel eyes that I could barely make out in his picture. Age 16.

It'll be my first time having a butler.

Linda Banks is my maid, from Farms. Long brown hair, olive skin, age 16 as well.

Stepping off the majestic staircase, I see Linda and Caleb standing at attention, their escorts behind them. The escorts bow and Caleb and Linda follow.

"Welcome to the palace," I greet Linda and Caleb. "You may rise." The escorts discreetly back away.

"It's an honor to serve, Your Highness," Linda says. I smile at her.

"I agree," Caleb chimes in. I shift my gaze to him and suddenly feel self-conscious in my burgundy dress and off-white lace shawl. He smiles warmly, however, and the feeling dissipates.

"Thank you. I'll be meeting with each of you one on one to discuss your duties," I say. "But first, I'll be showing you around the palace."

Caleb and Linda nod. "This way," I direct, walking to the edge of the Grand Hall. A guard opens a side door, and we walk down a small corridor I rarely see. "This is one of the servants' halls. There are lots of these that branch off from the servants' quarters, but you probably won't use them too often. You'll mostly be working in my room or your room. In case you do, however, there are supply closets around this area. Any questions?"

They both shake their heads, so I continue down the passage. Once we reach the servants' quarters, I say, "This is the servants' quarters. There's the mess hall where you'll eat meals, supply closets with whatever you might need for your jobs, and your rooms are just up here."

Caleb nods. Linda pipes up with a question. "Will we have roommates?"

"No, you have your own rooms," I say. "And Linda, your room is here. Number 9."

I push open the door to the small living space. "You can decorate with any personal items. There's a sleeping area, some storage space, and a work area. Caleb, your room is the same."

I glance across the dim hallway. I haven't been down here in a year, and I crane my neck to find Room 28 past the bustling servants.

"Oh, there it is." I close Linda's door and move purposefully through the crowd. The servants back out of my way with bows, and I acknowledge them with a nod. Reaching Caleb's door, I turn to him and Linda. "Caleb, your room is number 28. Again, any questions?"

Linda shakes her head. "No, but thank you," Caleb says.

I smile. "You're welcome. If you ever need anything, just tell me or Ma'am Marlene. She's the head of the staff. I believe she called you both before your arrival?" I continue at their nods. "I also have a smartscreen for you. You'll mainly use it for your duties and contacting me, but you can also contact your families or friends at home.

"Linda, would you mind meeting with me first?" I ask.

"Absolutely," she says.

"Excellent. Let's go to my room. Caleb, you can take time to get accustomed to your new room. I'll send for you when Linda and I are done talking."

Caleb nods and heads into his room, and I lead Linda up to the second floor, where the royal quarters are. My bedroom has three areas: the bedroom, the meeting room, and the bathroom. Linda and I take a seat at the sleek, long table in the meeting room. I usually sit at the head of the table, but I decide that would be too formal today. Instead, I sit in one of the half-dozen rolling chairs surrounding the table, Linda taking the spot across from me.

"So, you're from Farms. What work did you do?" I inquire.

"I was a seamstress. I made clothes for the Highs who lived near me," Linda says. Her words have a little sting of accusation, but it wasn't noticeable enough to prompt a reaction. I simply nod.

"That's good. You'll have several jobs as my maid, but working with clothes is a big part of your duties. First of all, you'll be helping me get ready every morning...." I tell her the words I've heard so many times. It used to be Ma'am Marlene, the head of staff, greeting the new servants while I stood by nervously. Now that I've come of age, it's my turn.

"And just anything else I need," I finish. "I really appreciate your service to the palace."

She smiles. "Thank you. May I be excused?"

She's the first of my servants that I can remember ever asking to leave. I admire her directness.

"Absolutely," I say. "Could you bring Caleb up to meet me? And ask him to bring his smartscreen, please."

I really should show him up to my room, but I've been frowned upon for visiting the servants' quarters lately. I squirm, remembering the judgmental glare of an advisor.

I check my smartscreen while waiting for Caleb. No new contacts or reminders—surprisingly.

Just as I slide the smartscreen into a hidden pocket in my dress, I hear a faint knock on the meeting room door. "Come in," I call.

Caleb slowly pushes open the door. "You can take a seat there," I say, pointing to the spot where Linda had sat. I squeeze my legs into my chair so they don't brush Caleb's.

“I wanted to ask, what work did you do in Ames?”

“My family farms,” he says.

I nod. If you look closely, it’s obvious he does manual labor.

“So you probably don’t know much about work as a butler.” He shakes his head. “Well, your duties are pretty simple. You’ll escort me to formal events, bring food to my room in case I need or want to eat in here, and help me with my schedule and events.”

I show him my schedule and explain the dining and escort processes.

“Any questions?” I finally say.

“You seem to ask that a lot,” he replies, smiling.

I sigh. “It’s my first time doing this orientation,” I admit. “I just don’t want you to feel lost.”

“I appreciate that,” he says. “I don’t have any, though. Questions, I mean. You did a good job explaining.”

“Thank you.” I smile. “I’ll see you later.”

With a bow, Caleb exits the room.

The orientation was draining, but I did it. I can do this.

“May I ask, what was going through your mind when you picked your servants at the Serving Ceremony?”

“I was concerned about my choice, but of course, it’s a lottery. I decided not to worry about whom I would draw and just choose.”

novel writing

Mom and Mum asked me to do an interview with *Cypress Weekly News* about the Serving Ceremony, for an "after the ceremony" segment. I agreed, but I'm nervous now, sweating under the bright lights in the Njano Parlor. Camera people drift around me and the reporter, a cheerful High woman named Lisa Walls.

"Can you tell us a little bit about Ms. Banks and Mr. Abrams?" she asks.

"Well, Mr. Abrams farmed. He's from Ames. Ms. Banks was a seamstress from Farms."

"How would you say you're getting along with them?"

"They're excellent! They've both done really well at the palace so far. Mr. Abrams and Ms. Banks are definitely people I can work with."

"That's great to hear. I also wanted to ask, the Servants' Ball is coming up in less than a week. How are you feeling about that?" Ms. Walls asks. The Servants' Ball is a ball to "celebrate the services of the palace staff." Everyone on the staff is off duty the night of the ball.

I paste on a smile. "I'm excited! I hope it shows the servants how much we appreciate them."

"Thank you," the woman says. I smile, and Ms. Walls waves off the cameras.

"You'll see this interview on the next weekly news segment, Your Highness," she tells me.

I nod. "Thank you."

My room is quiet, light streaming in from the open windows as I pick up my smartscreen and reading glasses. I need to finish figuring the military budget report, come up with an organization system for the climate schedules—today's a day to get stuff done.

I shove open my regular door, then turn around to use the connecting door I temporarily forgot about. My foot catches on something, and I tumble to the ground, my smartscreen and reading glasses flying in front of me.

"Oh my—are you okay?" a familiar voice frantically asks.

I pick myself up and brush off my clothes. "Yeah, I'm fine," I say, tucking my curls behind my ear before turning to face the voice.

It's Caleb, his face apologetic as he says, "I'm so sorry."

"It's fine," I reassure him, bending down to pick up my smartscreen and reading glasses. I look them over. No scratches. "What did you need?"

"I didn't want to ask Ma'am Marlene," he says, ducking his head. "It's just—I've never used a smartscreen. I don't know how to get to your calendar."

"Of course," I say, sighing. "I'm so sorry. I forgot to tell you and Linda about how the smartscreens work."

"I think Linda knows," Caleb says. "I've never used one, though."

“Here, come into my meeting room.” I gesture to the door to my right. “I’ll walk you through it.”

Caleb sits in the same spot as earlier, but this time I sit next to him and lean over as I demonstrate how to work the smartscreen.

“And this brings up the holographic keyboard, which is helpful for work,” I say. I reach across him to press the button, our arms touching for a second. “Sorry.”

Soon enough, I’ve gone through all the features I can think of.

“No questions,” Caleb says. “Before you ask.”

I smile.

Glancing at the clock, I realize I spent half an hour helping him, half an hour I could have spent on work. But I don’t really mind.

Chapter 5. Caleb

I use the back stairs to get back to my room, more confident about my smartscreen and the palace in general. I was worried Princess Nyeshi would be strict or cold, but she radiates kindness.

Opening the door to my room, I spot a packet on my small wooden table.

My room here is simple. There’s a wooden bed with white sheets and a thick brown blanket, a strange contrast to the blue and red quilt draped over my bed at home. On the wall opposite the table, metal hooks are bolted into the wall. Thin wire hangers dangle from the hooks, holding three identical pairs of my uniform.

It's a lot less crowded than my room at home, but it's far more lonely.

I pick up the packet and peel a sticky note off the front. "This is the Servants' Ball information packet," it reads. "The etiquette class is mandatory for new servants. Contact me or Princess Nyeshi with any questions."—Ma'am Marlene.

Flipping through the packet, I notice a section stating that Princess Nyeshi will present a traditional flower to me before the ball. The packet also lists the date and time for an etiquette class. "For servants to learn or review proper palace etiquette," it reads. The class is at noon tomorrow in the Njano Parlor, somewhere Princess Nyeshi didn't point out on the tour earlier. I'll have to ask her about it.

An angry tone comes from my smartscreen—I must have set the ringtone to something weird when Princess Nyeshi explained how to change it. I flip the smartscreen open to see the caller ID. Recognizing our home number, I swipe the green answer button.

"Caleb!" Adelia shrieks. "Oh, I missed you."

It's strange to see her face and hear her at the same time, but it's nice, too.

"Hi," I say with a smile. "I missed you too! Are you on a smartscreen?"

"Yeah. We got one with your salary."

"Wow. That's great!" We've gone from barely being able to afford eggs to getting a smartscreen. Maybe we'll even advance castes with this newfound wealth. It's doubtful—you have to be in the next caste's money range for two years before advancing. Still, it could happen.

I'm not sure how I'd feel about that.

"So, what's happening at the palace?" Adelia asks.

"We have to do an etiquette class before the Servants' Ball. I barely even know what etiquette means," I confess. "But Princess Nyeshi's really nice. And her maid, Linda, seems okay. I haven't really gotten to know anyone else yet."

"I'm sure you'll make friends," Adelia reassures me. "I'm glad the princess is nice. And don't worry about the Servants' Ball. It's for you to take a break and have fun, right?"

"I guess so."

Adelia glances over her shoulder. "What? Okay," she says, then turns back to me with an apologetic look. "I'm sorry, Caleb, but I have to go. We're behind on our assigned acre."

"That's fine," I say with a smile. "Good luck. See you soon."

She smiles. "Bye."

Amazing Grace

TYLER CATLIN

Grade 12. Sacred Heart School, Falls City, NE. Linda Kirkendall, Educator. Silver Key.

novel writing

Prologue

Alex was propped up against the wall in his room, reading when he heard the door slam shut. Even though he was fourteen he flinched when the house's door was slammed shut. "Stupid," he cursed himself for being so jumpy.

Even though he cursed himself, his fear was put in the right spot. The slammed door meant one of two things, most of the time. The first possibility as that one of his parents, or both, had come home mad. This scenario was enjoyed much more than the second, even though their anger normally got taken out on him. Alex seemed to be the perfect punching bag for them; he even made sounds when a good, solid punch would hit him. As bad as that sounds, the second possibility was worse.

Occasionally his parents would come home drunk, unable to reason and too blind to see if Alex couldn't take anymore. These instances chilled Alex to the bones. He could normally tell when they were drunk novel writing

and the fear of what was going to happen made the beating even worse. One of the tells that his parents had when they were drunk was their agility, normally swift and agile, became like that of a newborn ape. Even then they were dangerous, though. Their strength seemed to multiply as reason faded from their minds. If they managed to get a hold of Alex when they were drunk, he was almost as good as dead. Their minds had one thing in them: a rage so uncontrollable that only sobriety could control them.

After those second instances, Alex almost always ended up in the E.R. His parents didn't bring him there. That would raise suspicions, they thought. People would start to wonder if he was being abused. It seems like people happen to be smart that way. The person who would bring him to the hospital was the neighbor, Chan. Since the beginning of 2015, Alex had been to the hospital ten times. He was counting.

Every time that Chan would bring him to the hospital, stepping in front of the lumbering creatures that Alex knew as his parents, he risked his health. He seemed to be the only force capable of stopping his parents other than sobriety. Even with the fact that it was two on one, Chan never was afraid of Alex's parents. Chan always told Alex, "A man who is doing what is right knowingly will always beat an oppressive force that is not in its right mind."

As cool as Alex thought the saying was, he never understood it. The only response he ever gave Chan after the times he would impart that saying on Alex was a simple dismissive smile and a shake of the head. The saying didn't make sense; there were millions of scenarios in which Alex could picture the oppressive force beating the good man. If the man had to fight a dragon that was more fearsome than any creature that Tolkien could fabricate. If the man was shot by a sniper as he walked through the streets of a town to confront a powerful dictator. If the man was fighting an army and was taken off guard. The list went on and on, each one ending in the defeat of the good man. Chan was never in any of those situations, though, so Alex guessed the saying did make sense for him at least. Until the day only months ago when Chan should have been afraid. When Chan should have known that someday, knowing right or not, he should have had fear of at least one unstoppable force.

While Alex was thinking of Chan he sat with his back to the wall, sitting deathly still. He didn't read anymore. His eyes were fixated on the hall outside his door, waiting to see a shadow. His legs were pushing him tightly against the wall, straining to keep him as far from the door as possible. "Please don't be mad or drunk. Please just accidentally have shut the door too strongly. Please. Please," Alex whimpered, no longer cursing himself as his fears grew in his mind.

There was a crash in the kitchen. Among the noise Alex could hear a glass object shatter. Shortly after the clatter, there was a roar that filled the house. "Oh, no. Oh, no," Alex squeaked in between gulps of fear.

"*Alex!*" his dad yelled, his voice a harsh whip through the air. The window in Alex's room rattled as the strength of his voice collided with the glass panel.

Shaking, Alex got up. Shaking in anticipation of the beating that he knew waited just down the hall and to the right, he started to walk toward the door, gulping almost constantly. He hoped against hope that Chan would show up. He hoped against hope that nothing would happen other than a stern conversation.

Walking down the hall, though, Alex knew that neither of those would happen with a sort of fatal certainty. Before he turned into the kitchen he swallowed that fact and tried to prepare for what would come next. As he entered he was ready, but not ready at all for the beating that followed.

How Sweet the Sound

The beating that had taken place was on the day before the school year started. His dad must have forgotten himself amongst his anger and lashed out too much, too hard. The parents seemed to have an unspoken rule that they wouldn't visibly hurt him when the wound would be very apparent and fresh during the school day, so most of the time they did hidden punches to the gut, belt lashes against the back, kicks to his butt. Areas that wouldn't be seen in public, this way they still got their punching bag but didn't get them reported to child protective services. Still, his dad had gotten carried away and now his black hair was accented by shades of purple that covered half of his face.

It wasn't the worst beating that he had ever received, and it helped that his dad was sober. Alex had some hidden thanks in his heart that his dad wasn't drunk just because he knew that if his dad had been drunk his beating would have been that much worse.

He had left his house early to account for the previous night's beating and so that he could get out of the house. Alex thought about the night before as he walked across the small town of Plaintill to get to school. His gait had an obvious limp; his right leg had gotten the worst of the beating. That wasn't bad, jeans covered all signs except for the limp but nobody would be able to tell what it was from. His book bag was slung over his shoulder, sagging and nearly bursting at the seams with his school supplies and library books that were stuffed inside of it. His walk was quiet and peaceful. The street lights were still on and barely another soul was moving.

He finally got to the school after walking eight blocks. His hair had fallen into his eyes and he pushed it aside so that he could check the time on the watch, a nice one with a leather band, steel frame, and blue face, that Chan had given him the previous year for Christmas. It was six o' one. He still had time to read a bit before the first teachers would arrive and unlock the building. The simple thought of reading made a smile come to his face.

That smile was replaced with a grimace as he turned and limped a couple blocks east of the school to his favorite park. While the town had three parks, each one as beautiful as the last, the one close to the school, Hansch Park, was his favorite. The park had no playground and Alex hoped that it would stay that way so that the natural beauty and peace of it would stay preserved.

The park used to be a section of land owned by a family known as the Hansches. The Hansch family was a very nature-loving family and was known for traveling across the country to visit state parks and camp. The park was beautiful in that it reflected that aspect of their personality.

The park had been built after Herman Hansch's wife, Emily, died. She was the one who had been the most adventurous of the family and had always vouched that Plaintill needed an actual park that would capture the beauty of nature. Many thought that the park was a sad place since Emily had never gotten to see it.

Alex always shook his head when he heard people talk about the park like that. He hadn't known Emily Hansch, but he had read the short biography of her life that the park had at its entrance more than enough times to feel like he had known her. Since everything in the park had been dedicated to her he figured that she was a wonderful woman who knew what true beauty looked like. She was probably kind and would have been the woman who gave out lots of candy to little kids during Halloween. She had probably been strong, too, and had stood up for the little man. He'd had lots of time to daydream about what type of person she was.

The dedicatee aside, the park was still a wonderful place. The plans for it had been drawn by Emily. There was a picture of the sketch that the park was designed by at the same spot where the biography on her life was. It had been a plain sketch, just a few details had been added, but somehow you could see the sheer amount of imagination that she had put into the park. A lake rested in the middle of the park. On the middle of the lake was an island that geese would often inhabit as a safe place from most predators. A sidewalk, and the only thing that truly looked man-made in the entire park except for a few benches, circled the lake and ventured off at parts so that you could view the other parts of the park. Trees bushes and flowers had been planted in set areas but had been left to grow where they pleased. Even though the park's wildlife was very free from constraints, the Hansch family tended the vegetation so that it would still look as though somebody cared about it.

Alex had never been outside of Plaintill, except for a few field trips, and it was this park that had made him come to see that nature was beautiful. He longed to go camping, just so that he could experience nature the way that the Hansches had.

He sat on his favorite bench and opened his book. Before he started reading he mumbled, "Nothing wrong here." The sun had started to come up and there was light to read with. The pages were illuminated with a faint glow that made them seem ancient. The book may as well have been; it was a classic that was printed who knows when and it hadn't been kept in the best condition at the library.

The story was intriguing. He hadn't read a book like it before. Most of the stories he read were horror, fantasy, or mystery. This story was somewhat historical yet also fictional. He loved how the author wrote it and knew somewhere deep in his heart that he wouldn't be able to find another historical fiction book that captured him like this one had.

The world that he entered when he read the book was amazing. It wasn't so much the fact that it was better but that it was created almost to the minutest detail. Every detail took his senses and described a scene in nature that made the town that circled the park he read in seem so far away. The best detail that was added, or forgotten, was that his parents weren't in the book and neither were his beatings.

That was his favorite part. In the story he got to read it from the point of view of a character that had a loving family. For the short time that he would read he got to find out what it was like to have a family who cared about him. It helped him cope.

It seemed like the more that he thought about his reading helping him, the more that he thought of it as a coping mechanism. When he read he could escape his world, his harsh reality, and his pain, leaving them for a happier, less painful, more hopeful world and reality. The worlds that had happy endings in them, the worlds that the hero won and the bad guys lost. Worlds where children's parents would love them back.

Alex envied those kids when he thought about them after putting the book down. That didn't matter, though. He knew that no matter how much envy he would have, his parents wouldn't reflect his love for them.

He used to bring his situation up to his classmates and his elementary teachers. They never believed him, though. "They just have different ways of showing that they love you," was their response almost every time.

Eventually it got into Alex's mind that his parents did love him, just differently. That illusion lasted long enough for him to gain common sense and see through the façade his teachers had put up in his mind.

When the realization hit, it was too late for him. He had learned to love his parents, even with the constant beatings. Somehow he started to believe that his parents, strong as they were, wouldn't last if he told on them. He wanted them to be safe. Somehow he got into his mind that if he left them one day and ran away, they wouldn't be able to live with each other because they would take their anger out on each other. He wanted them to at least love each other.

Over time, as Alex got older and out of his clumsy awkward stage and his bruises and scrapes remained, the teachers began to get a little suspicious. They would ask him every once in a while what had happened, to which he would respond that he had fallen on his way home from school the previous day. For some reason he began trying to find some way to throw the teachers off his case. It might have been that somewhere he knew that if anyone knew what his parents did to him they would end up in jail, and for the life of him he couldn't figure out why he felt deep in his gut that it would be a bad thing.

His chance to prove, to the teachers and himself, the innocence of his parents came the year that it started to get really bad. The chance came in eighth grade English when his class had to do a "Who is My Hero?" speech. He thought that maybe if he could write a speech about his parents being great role models and how they were incredibly loving, he could believe it too. It didn't work for him, but it did seem to work for the teachers. He had thought of all the times when his parents hadn't been awful to him and magnified those points so much that his parents seemed like angels. After that, his teachers were sold on the idea that his parents were great people. Alex felt proud of himself for being able to save his parents from what he thought would have been almost a fatal stay in that iron-barred hotel called *prison*.

Was that incredibly weird for an abused boy to do? Possibly, but Alex loved them. He felt like he owed them something for giving him life, for giving him shelter, for feeding him half-decent food. Even if his parents didn't love him it didn't stop him from loving them back for providing for him when they didn't have to. For that fact, Alex loved his parents with every fiber in his body. Even though they hurt him and beat him almost every night, he loved them with every broken and fractured bone in his body. He thought that he couldn't hate them. Somehow, he knew that if he couldn't hate them then he was probably incapable of hate.

He lost track of time as he read on the bench that overlooked the pond in the middle of the park. A person who was out for a jog jolted him back to reality. He glanced at his watch and read the time: half past seven. Hurriedly he marked his spot in the book, put his book in his bag, and stood up, temporarily forgetting his pain. The pain wasn't going to let him forget that quickly, though, and a wave of pain almost knocked him on his butt. He wobbled for a second before grabbing his book bag and hoisting it onto his shoulder. After that he limped as fast as his legs would allow him back to the school.

If he got to the school late enough, the halls were crowded and he would have trouble navigating the halls. That fact and the fact that more crowded halls meant it would be likely that he would be seen if the jocks of the school decided to kick off the school year by kicking him. Those were the reasons that he went to school early. If he went early, nobody else was there. If no one else was there, he would attract no unwanted attention and would be able to coast through the day without attracting that unwanted attention.

At the Crossing

Olivia Achtemeier

Grade 11. Beatrice High School, Beatrice, NE. Meghan Robeson, Educator. Gold Key.

From a distance, the train appears to be gliding,
as if it has not a care in the world.
It gracefully flows through the forest,
then wistfully strolls in the fields.
I draw nearer.

She cries out in fear,
running in a great escape.
Her gray, billowing hair trails behind her,
and without ceasing, she presses on.
I draw nearer once more.

The prideful beast plows through the crossing,
with no regard for the impatient animals below.
The herd follows each precise movement,
all gallantly carrying faded colors.
I hold my breath, waiting for it to pass.

The arms that bring me to a halt are now lifted,
while I gaze at the mountainous creature in a detached
state.

poetry

Gradually the herd becomes nothing more than a mere
speck,
eventually, its wild sounds fill my ears no longer.
I dutifully, yet clumsily bump over the beast's tracks.

poetry

The High Horse

Olivia Achtemeier

Grade 11. Beatrice High School, Beatrice, NE. Meghan Robeson, Educator. Silver Key.

I gaze up at the ones who hurt me.
Beside each of them stands a single horse,
With a beautiful coat and flowing mane.
I look into its eye: glazed over but welcoming.
I carefully mount myself and observe my surroundings;
There's an entire field covered with those sitting still on horses,
Some horses taller, some horses shorter.

I hear the mocking of others once again,
So I look at my horse and admire it.
In an instant, the horse shoots up a foot or two.
Another calls at me and sees my faults,
So I brush the mane of my horse.
In a moment, the horse gains height.
Time after time, the insults come, but my horse continues to grow.

I look at the field once more,
Covered with horses, though something's changed.

poetry

poetry

I no longer gaze up, but rather peer down.
The field is surrounded by horses and their riders,
Yet everyone is alone.
I squint at the ground below, afraid to return.
I lower my head, ashamed of what I've become.

Jumping from my horse, I gaze up one last time.
The insults continue to come,
But I refuse to climb back on.
I now see what I'd ignored before:
The horse is covered in mud and its eyes speak of
deceit.
I walk away from what had been so hard to get down
from.
I abandon the high horse.

The Window Sill

Olivia Achtemeier

Grade 11. Beatrice High School, Beatrice, NE. Meghan Robeson, Educator. Silver Key.

From just below my window sill, people rush from one street to another.
Some share friendly 'ellos, while others glance to and fro.
Some are absorbed in a phone call, while others seem to have no cares at all.
Some run and look distraught, while others walk leisurely with supplies they bought.
I frown from where I sit, contemplating all of this.
Why do we go so fast as if we've had enough with chance?
How much of our lifetime is spent without content?
I've seen first-hand one without any demand.
It wasn't what was collected, but rather about perspective.
Anything held was only to give, and gave out of the joy of being saved.

poetry

Only a moment's pause, and I find my gaze downward
yet again.
One small boy stands, overwhelmed as if it's all so
grand.
One street performer plays, he sings the songs of yes-
terday.
One mother holds her own with a smile, deciding
there's time to sit a while.
My face brightens, and with a breath my chest light-
ens.
Was this something I missed, there's still great bliss?
Had my mind been booked without these details I'd
overlooked?
Upon my hands I rest my head, a grin replaces my
expression of dread.
A lovely memory graces my mind, a person who was
one of a kind.
I recall the one that passed, but never from below my
window sill.

poetry

Identity, A Prose Poem

Tanya Bachu

Grade 9. Brownell Talbot School, Omaha, NE. Matt Low, Educator. Honorable Mention.

Tanya. Deeply transcendental. Thoroughly in tune with the divine. Spending time, solely. Beholding philosophical, pious, and spiritual motives in an endeavor to find authentic truth. Sagacious, but often exuding mystery as if tapped into something others won't understand. Alfresco. Convalescing with nature. Perpetually seeking to understand existence, placement within the macrocosm, and life's mysteries. Artistic and poetic. Keenly observing with high perspicacity, the human condition. Mystical. Sapient. Eccentric. Intuitive. Tanya.

We Gather Here Today for the Death of Words

Ashley Binstock

Grade 12. Bishop Neumann Central High School, Wahoo, NE. Marisa Grady, Educator.

Portfolio Gold Key

poetry

I want words to die
They are wrong
Twisted up
Corrupted outlines
Of what I am trying to say
They mean nothing crumbling into the shadow of my heart
My heart that is *screaming* louder than my tongue
Its pulse drowning out the toneless vibration of air
I must be listened to
And yet words don't allow me to be heard
They are frail phrases dissolving against the midnight of my pain
I want to bury them under the realization that I am catastrophically desperate to burst
And I am afraid if not in words
In **Flame**

Alphabet Soup

Ashley Binstock

Grade 12. Bishop Neumann Central High School, Wahoo, NE. Marisa Grady, Educator.

Portfolio Gold Key

Letters.
Letters marching
Swirling in a mush of spindly strings around my soul
When did alphabet soup grow limbs
and sentences
and declarations
When did pieces of spaghetti become weapons in war
The delicate chains shaved into precise targets
I miss the way they used to shimmer
The times they swam and danced and twirled
I'm sick of how they have been squashed into
judgments
and rumors
and silence
When did the pasta turn cold in our bellies
And put blood on our tongues

poetry

Two Fears

Ashley Binstock

Grade 12. Bishop Neumann Central High School, Wahoo, NE. Marisa Grady, Educator.

Portfolio Gold Key

poetry

You say you are afraid like it is only air leaving your
 lungs
Like those three words have stained your freshly
 washed blouse
And you can't help but grumble against the bad luck

I say I am afraid like I am plummeting
The air rushing past my ears in deafening waves
As I loom toward the ever-impending ground

Like a switch has gone off in my brain and suddenly
I cannot breathe and be afraid at the same time
I cannot hear beneath the roar of thoughts

You do not understand my afraid

You will never understand my afraid
Because you are too busy scrubbing
At the stain on your blouse

Its Questions

Mary Blankenship

Grade 12. Fort Calhoun Junior Senior High School, Fort Calhoun, NE. Sara Gross, Educator. Honorable Mention.

I give it 6 months.
Pregnant? Are you serious?!
She wonders why I left.
Cannabis
Untrustworthy
The money that came from my father? Don't you
remember?
No, you don't. You smoked it all already
And then, after four years of fighting, I got what I
wanted.
I moved, living with my father.
I couldn't anymore. So much would change, right?

A true name? A true thought?
Struggling to make it through the day
Forcing myself to stay awake. No sleep availed last
night with the strained yelling and *BANG* ... *thud*
What was that noi—? *Would you stop yelling at me for
one goddamn second?!*
"It's Your kid. Not mine!"

poetry

... it's your kid

it's

But was it ever important? Seems more inconvenient
than anything.
It sits, day in, day out.
"Stop sleeping from after school until 10pm!"
But he doesn't know the reason it sleeps
It sleeps because it correlates emotion with the demons
The demons joust and snarl, fighting for a way into the
mind.
They won.

Well ... are you happy now?
It is gone. It isn't a burden anymore. It only needed a
trigger. Guess what?
The screaming couple? That was the emotional trigger.
"I can't do this anymore!" And you think I could,
alone?
After the innermost trigger, it only needed the clicking
one.
One bullet in the chamber
Now none

I've finally solved the unfathomable.
It was the problem. No problem remains. Maybe now
you'll notice.

Poetry Trio

Mary Blankenship

Grade 12. Fort Calhoun Junior Senior High School, Fort Calhoun, NE. Sara Gross, Educator. Silver Key.

"More Than Wounded Hearts"

I can hear the beating hearts of the
    Young men and women that are losing lives
Slam. Bang. Clank.
I can see the tears, the mothers cry
    After finding out what happened
I'm so sorry, ma'am.
I can feel the panic rushing through the children's
    bodies as that alarm blares
Tick. Tock. Click. Click.
I can sense the fear leaking from their body
    as they debate whether they are next
Mrs. Willa, what's going on?
And as that door opens and those children
    send their last text
"I love you, Mom and Dad. No matter what."
And I can hear weapons drawn and children screaming
    Then silence

poetry

poetry

"Teddy's Mourn"

The teddy bear lay on the bed
Waiting for the little girl to come home
He thought to himself, "it's almost time"
And he would be with his girl again

Seconds to days, suns to moons
She doesn't make an appearance
He starts to listen to see if he can hear her
Not a peep, a snicker, not even a tap

When he hears nothing, absolute silence
He starts to worry and cry out loud
The mother bursts through in tears, grabs him,
And cuddles the super soft bear

While his tears drip down his fuzzy cheeks
He knew the girl wasn't going to return

"Beginning Flicker"

A candle ablaze lit in the dark
All it took was a single spark
As hours go by, the flame, it dims
And as it goes out I hear angel hymns

There they are, so faint, so sweet
The child inside of me gently weeps
The angels came down and took her away
Like father, like daughter; I am left astray

I was so honored to deliver a life
Even though we weren't man and wife
And even after the depression and strain
Hopefully some day I get to try again

Hopefully my candle will light again

poetry

A Bit of Solace

Victoria Bogatz

Grade 8. Lewis & Clark Middle School, Bellevue, NE. Michelle Kastl, Educator. Gold Key.

poetry

A bit of solace
The night is dark and deep
And it's been far too long
The stars are gone
What else to do
But drive quietly
Along empty roads
The fields swaying slightly

I stare, as if
Some lost hope
Tangible peace
Is hiding in the goldenrods

Alone with my thoughts
I am no longer lost
Just a wanderer
Gravel crunching below my tires

A bird whistles from afar

That's when I feel it
Maybe not joy
But a bit of solace
And that's enough

poetry

Silver Linings

Gabrielle Burns

Grade 8. Home School, Gretna, NE. Jaime Burns, Educator. Silver Key.

Paradise

The way the wind blows gently rustling my hair,
The warm spring breeze with traces of summer's air.
Every sound a symphony, every silence a rest,
Every movement a dance, every creature a guest.
The stars shine like embers in the sky,
And the man in the moon smiles from his place up
high.
Every scent is sweet like the roses in the wind,
Like the cherry blossoms whose flowers are never
dimmed.
I know this version of the world is never hard to find,
This perfect place exists in fragments in my mind.

Easy! careful mind.

Easy! Careful mind.
Let the waves come to bay.
Let the searching find,
And the day slip away.
Quiet! Noisy head.

Let an echo fill the space.
Lay still upon the bed,
And find peace and grace.
Still. Active brain.
Stop worrying about tomorrow.
Let peace fall like rain,
In this second that I borrow.
Come, peaceful rest.
Let me slip away.
Take me in as your guest,
Until there is a new day.

Storm

The rain knocks on the cold window,
And the lamplight casts its yellow glow.
The sky is black, the shade of the berry,
There's a calming feeling, it's oddly merry.
The whole world looks fresh and new,
Out the window I am looking through.
The thunder rolls with a gentle crash,
After a bright lightning flash.
For seconds the sky is painted with streaks of silver,
You can see its reflection on the street's shallow river.
On the inside I am calm and warm,
But outside there is a thunderstorm.

The Walk

I roam the streets without a care.
The sound of silence fills the air.
I hear a steady rhythm, a pounding beat,
The sound of cement against my feet.
As I walk along I see a bird,
Which appears to be speaking without using words.
I smell an aroma so pure, so clean,
It makes me forget everything mean.
I feel like a bird with wings to soar,
I want this feeling just one day more.
I taste an imaginary taste so clean, so sweet,
A taste I never thought I'd come to meet.
The wind sings a song, which seems to say,
nothing could ruin this perfect day.

poetry

Silver Linings

Seeing the rose in a bush of thorns,
Seeing the night as a bridge to the morn.
A caterpillar, a future butterfly,
An answer, in a million questions why.
A new place, a fresh start,
Freedom in a broken heart.
It's not that I see an imperfect world for something it's not,
It's just that I don't see the good in giving it my thought.
In a cloud that blocks the sun from shining,
A silver lining.

My Protector, Paranoia

Ana Carson

Grade 9. Doniphan-Trumbull High School, Doniphan, NE. Stacey McCarty, Educator. Silver Key.

I was born with an extra voice in my head
One of anxiety and fear
At a young age
I could never understand what this voice was
Why was it telling me all these things to worry my little adolescent mind about
As I grew, the voice did too
It took over my head
It went from a whisper to a bellow
I started to feel it was my friend
My protector of all things that I feared
It told me what was safe
What I was allowed to do
The voice always won over my brain
At 10 I was checking that all doors were locked
and then rechecking again
At 11 I wouldn't sleep by a window
as eyes are everywhere
And I could almost feel a hand creeping along my trembling body
At 12 I slept in the corner of my room every night

poetry

because that's the only way I could see who was coming in the door
and who was hiding in my closet
the mornings I woke up with my back sore from the hard ground were all worth it when I woke up alive
At 13 I was barging into my little brother's room to check if he was breathing
The picture I had seen in my head fresh in my mind
he was stiff, cold, and as still as I had seen him in his five years of life
At 14 I would sleep with the light on
because that coat rack looks like a figure
I swear I could make out a face
and its hands reaching out to seize me
wrapping around my neck
Now at 15 I can't sleep a full night
because the voice lets a new sick fairytale seep into my head every night
and every one stays with me
because it's another vision the voice haunts me with
If I'm walking at night, and someone is across the street
I must walk toward the lights
Because the voice isn't telling me to be scared of that person
It tells me to be scared of what a person is capable of
If my grandma sleeps late

I tiptoe into her room to see her chest move up and
down
Because the voice tells me
it was her time
The voice is my protector
My friend
But
It's also my foe
My rival
Who takes over my life
My choices
And makes me a weak prey among the world
Stuck with the fear of living
I'm only surviving
Paranoia is not the fear of something there
It's the fear of *what could be there,*
what it can do,
the possibilities
I'm not scared of heights
I'm scared of *slipping down*
I'm not scared of drowning
I'm scared of *feeling my breath get taken out of my body*
I'm not scared of strangers
I'm scared *of being taken apart*
piece
by
piece

poetry

I'm not scared of life
I'm scared of the capabilities of it
How quickly it can take everything
Paranoia
My buddy
My pal
Can you visit someone else
Some poor soul in need of protecting
I want to live
I want to have my teenage years
because you took my childhood
I no longer need your voice guiding me through the world
I need strength to become part of it
To be a member of this society
15 years of protection
Yet somehow
I still don't feel safe
And it's all because
I was born with an extra voice in my head

An Account of a Modern-Day Ethiopian

Megan Lambert

Grade 11. Boys Town High School, Boys Town, NE. Beth Sulley, Educator. Gold Key. American Voices Nominee.

poetry

what kind of strength you contain
to raise a family
in the midst of a war-struck country
knowing that another is raising your eldest daughter
in a land of plenty

you ignore your hunger pains
as you wipe your youngest daughter's tears away
rocking her to sleep
as bullets erupt just beyond your window

you tell her that the loud sound is heavenly thunder
that God is having a party up above
yet struggle to answer how there can be thunder
and the absence of rain

she asks you, in the quiet voice you love,
where is God?
she cannot find him in the streets
as news of rebels, crimes, and war is no longer new

it has become normal
where is God?

you kiss her cheek
and place your hand above her heart
God is here
and there in the world
you reply
some people just need help seeing Him

she closes her eyes after saying a prayer
when she is heavy with sleep
you tuck her in bed
before going to yours

you awake to a new day
braiding your little girl's hair
until you can't feel the tips of your fingers
her cloud of curls now tamed

you hold her hand as you walk through the city
bending down to kiss her head
whispering a prayer in her ear
watching her scramble into the rundown building they
call a school
you say another prayer when she is out of sight

on your way back home
you pass military officers with ashen faces
and worn Ethiopian flags
they nod at you

as if a single nod
could erase the fighting
less than 300 miles from where you stand

you nod back at them
they look just as the whole nation feels—tired

as you enter your home
you realize you were holding your breath

you clean your house
even though it is already clean
before moving on to your daily work
you allow yourself to be absorbed
by the tasks at hand

you realize that morning
has faded into afternoon
on your way to walk your youngest daughter home
you pass by the orphanage you last held your
eldest daughter in

poetry

you don't think you will ever forget the day
she walked into another's life
to be raised just as their own
leaving you empty handed
but with a selfless heart full of love

you stand at the entrance of the school
your little girl runs into your arms
dropping her books at your feet
you pick her up and squeeze her
she squeals and you laugh

she looks just like you
exactly like your other daughter did at her age

you blink twice and grasp her hand
tucking her books beneath your arm
you walk through the crazed streets
as if you were a warrior
unfazed by all the chaos

a strong warrior you are
to raise a family
in a country poisoned by a civil war

Dear

Megan Lambert

Grade 11. Boys Town High School, Boys Town, NE. Beth Sulley, Educator. Gold Key.

Dear Mom,
She wrote
She erased it to write

Dear Mother,
But that didn't feel right either
So she erased it again

Dear ...
She couldn't figure out what to call
This *lady* who failed to raise her
This *woman* who was supposed to protect her
This *person* who should've been more present
This *character* who should've acted as a parent

Dear
What would she write next?
She chose not to dwell in the past,
She preferred not to wallow in self pity, reliving the
events that had taken place

poetry

Dear
The lack of a title brought tears to her eyes
She didn't want to think that she did not have a
mother
That she lost out on something she never really had
Like the days they could've gone out for coffee or
gotten their nails done together

Dear
She put down her pencil
She didn't have anything else to say
So she left it at

Dear

Distance to Unity

Megan Lambert

Grade 11. Boys Town High School, Boys Town, NE. Beth Sulley, Educator. Silver Key.

I stand before you today
On a path that was paved by the leaders before me
A path that was weathered by change and defined by
  many
As an outlet, a platform for us all
So that we can cancel division and grow inclusivity
So that we can achieve a society affected by unity

Let us stand together for change
Working together to tackle adversity

For change cannot be sparked by a group
Who demands change but does not stand up for it

Let us stand side by side
Putting all of our differences aside
Making our community a sanctuary of pride
Because we reflect how distance turns into unity,
How people from every background in our country
Can stand together and embrace opportunity

As we progress right out of this era of inequality
Moving on from the stereotypes and racist trends
It is up to us to create new norms
It is up to us to decide the course of our futures
    together

The path we must pave for all who will come after us
Is the same, the same path that lies before us

So as I stand before you today
Let me ask you,
Do you stand with me?

The Life Cycle of Our One-Sided Life

Megan Lambert

Grade 11. Boys Town High School, Boys Town, NE. Beth Sulley, Educator. Honorable Mention.

you loved me first
I was the daughter you dreamed of
though I'm sure my actions sometimes made you
    question that
you provided everything I needed
you did your best to get me everything I wanted

you loved me first
I guess I knew you loved me
though those words never left your mouth to fill that
    void
sometimes I'd make you so angry you'd snap
I'm not sure how the words that left either of
our mouths reflected love
and for years I held on to that

you loved me first
our love dwindled before it went out as a dying flame
maybe it was the ember that I chased

poetry

that sparked the hope of a second chance
but just as embers do,
your love for me faded

I loved you second
maybe our circumstances are to blame
I know that if I loved you then, nothing would be the
same

you loved me first

I loved you second

but only our one-sided love remains

The Tulsa Massacre

Megan Lambert

Grade 11. Boys Town High School, Boys Town, NE. Beth Sulley, Educator. Silver Key.

I could smell the fire before I could see it
The smoke clouded the air as I scrambled out of my
room
I tripped my way out of the maze called my home,
Into a street lined by burning houses

Everything I knew and loved,
Everything familiar was up in flames
The destruction seemed endless,
The number of victims, unknown

We wandered through our broken city, Mama, Poppy,
and I
Anger flashed before my eyes, reflected in the fire

I clasped my trembling hand into Mama's
Wrapping my arm around Poppy's waist
I saw the fear inside her eyes
I read the uncertainty on his face

The grown adults mumbled words
Something about "Black Wall Street" and "burned to
the ground"
I thought I knew what those words meant
All I had to do was look around

My parents moved us into a tent
This tent made me miss my home
The newspapers said that it was entirely our fault
That our pain was just our own

poetry

I asked Poppy why we didn't have our home
What this was all about
I asked him if it was the white ghosts' fault
He said he thought it was

That the color of our skin makes some people afraid
This made me confused,
To me, we all seem the same

He replied, others are full of doubt
They are afraid of what they do not understand

When people are uncomfortable,
They reject the morals that they know
They cross the lines from right to wrong
To destruct everything that is different

Poppy explained that one day I won't have to be afraid
For I would live to see a time of change
A day when colored people, like me, are free

He spoke of a time that I would see
Where Greenwood would be restored
Where the bustling, glittering streets that I once knew
Would replace the rubble that stands today

I looked at my Poppy holding on to Mama
And I walked into their firm embrace
Inspired by their mighty faith
Amazed at how they believed that this day would come
While surrounded by our city of ruins

It would be years until change did come
About a hundred years or so
They now call the deaths, destruction, and lies, a
massacre
Because a riot was not what it was

The people of this day and age
Assure me that justice will be done
Now I'm sure it will
Just like my Poppy was

When I Was Your Everything

Megan Lambert

Grade 11. Boys Town High School, Boys Town, NE. Beth Sulley, Educator. Gold Key.

I consumed your life for a year
before you even met me
you filled out paperwork for hours, weeks, and months
back when I was your everything

the adoption agency seemed more like your friend
    than a company
you invited them over to your house frequently
they sat in your living room showing you pictures of
    me
and you say you instantly fell in love
back when I was your everything

it was a picture of me
that you proudly showed all of your friends and family
you even put it on your classroom desk
to remind you, on hard days, to keep going
you looked at me, though through a sheet of paper,
    with love
back when I was your everything

poetry

you held me in a cautious hug
when you met me in the orphanage that day
maybe you realized we both were so fragile
it was ultimately love that would make us break
but you loved me anyway
back when I was your everything

poetry

Cliché Love

Sky Lambrecht

Grade 12. Bellevue East Senior High School, Bellevue, NE. Trish Swoboda, Educator. Gold Key.

poetry

They say love is cliché.
It's worn and overused,
Battered and bruised.
But beautiful.

They say love burns brightly,
A warmth of being held tightly.
It lights the way for lovers to
Join their star-crossed paths.

They say love forms
Butterflies in stomachs
Of anxious, young lovers,
Flapping their wings high above others.

That's what they say.

If love is cliché,
Like they say,
Then where is *my* butterfly?
Why is there no flapping?

My orange monarch
Is shredded and beheaded
And dead.
And its royal reign is ruined.

The butterfly's golden crown
Is stripped to silver.
Its chrysalis throne
Is overthrown.

And I suffer the dictatorship of a Moth,
Blinded by a weakness of light.
Burdened with a grief of *my* submission,
It becomes love at first sight.

I must conform to the Moth.
Its flapping becomes thrashing.
The Moth cannot stomach living in my stomach.
So It *forces* my thoughts.

Like the Moth falls victim to a flame
I fall victim to the Moth.
I look to see perfection
And am burned by rejection.

They say love blossoms
Like bouquets of red roses.

poetry

A delicate, flourishing romance
That makes the heart want to dance.

They say love has petals of perfection.
A Romeo and Juliet.
Two attracted opposites,
Young when they first met.

They say love must be worn
With a heart on a sleeve.
A fruitful, mutual sacrifice
By an Adam and an Eve.

That's what they say.

But love is not cliché,
Like they say.
Why must I choose a crimson petal
In a flower field of rainbow?

These perfect, flourishing Roses
Wilt and wither with willingness.
Their reds dull to black
And they feel like their color won't come back.

Although they want sunshine,
They acknowledge the winter.

The Roses say they're fine,
They lie.

Their thorns once cut others.
But now the cold has cut *Them.*
They bend to the ground with submission,
Conforming is Their mission.

They bow their heads in silence.
Loneliness has won.
When They cry Their last desperate tears,
Their final petal is gone.

I hold Their hands, Their thorns.
The Roses slowly cut my confidence.
The red blood on my hand resembles the Roses.
And redless Daisies go unnoticed.

They say love is cliché.
It repeats with passion,
Remains in fashion.
And everyone seems to have it.

They say love is what gives
A happily ever after.
A happy heart beating
To the music of laughter.

They say love lasts forever.
"'Til death do us part"
Is the *part* people seem to praise.
Soulmates until a person's final days.

That's what they say,
That love is cliché.
But they forget
No one's love is the same.

Love is not battered and bruised,
Worn and over-used,
But rather my *self*
That remains beaten and unmoved.

I don't know how to find love.
How to nurture it into a butterfly.
It is stuck in its cocoon,
A breathless young prince without a tune.

I cannot flourish my rose
For fears it will rot.
Its sickly seed is saddened
And it falters below my nose.

There is no metamorphosis
No growth or change.

No perfect petals or radiant roses.
There is no photosynthesis.

Love is *not* cliché.

poetry

Comments of Aphrodite

Sky Lambrecht

Grade 12. Bellevue East Senior High School, Bellevue, NE. Trish Swoboda, Educator. Gold Key.

poetry

In the ancient days
Hopeless romantics looked to Aphrodite
To guide them in prosperous love
Primarily between man and woman.
She would intertwine them
Using an amorous belt around the two
Until their relationship grew
And they could express the feelings that they felt.
Some would pray to be closer to another
While others sought aid in fertility.
The mighty gods did not see her as much
Lacking respect for her,
Placing her promiscuity over her ingenuity.
But she was seen as an object
A nude, unattainable beauty and adulterer.
Her honor was washed away like her sea foam
Origin on the shores of Cyprus.
As she made love to Ares
She won beauty contests.
Aphrodite would show her true power.
She would be uncontested.

Just as she protected, guided, loved
Her forbidden mortal lovers in the Trojan war,
She remains present today.

"It will be okay."

She says as she makes posters
Of protest.
The sights of couples:

Man with woman
Man with man
Woman with woman
Anything in between

As the goddess of beauty,
She thinks of herself.
A beautiful rose
Crimson red.
A scenery of clouds above her head.
She cannot begin to compare her own beauty
To the beauty of this sight.
Of true love and compassion.
This makes her want to fight.
Her sign is a rainbow of colors
Each color symbolic of pride

"Love is love!"

Is written in bold.
She happily sings words of encouragement
To the rainbow of soldier protesters
Who fight alongside her,
Searching for liberty and love for all.
They don't see her of course, but they feel love in the air.
The army of prideful protesters
March for the freedom to love whomever
A person wishes.
To them, it's not black and white.
Love is love, and it should be everyone's right.

Man with woman
Man with man
Woman with woman
And anything in between

To them, love is more than gender, race, or sexuality.
Together, they fight, they protest against the brutality
Working against stigmas, for better mentalities
For those who can't in other countries.

Some can get killed for loving who they want
So Aphrodite stands for love

And refuses to sit until love is justified for all.
The crowd of people protesting for love
Sing and chant around and above.

But Aphrodite is suddenly saddened,
And the blue of the rainbow becomes more overwhelming.
She sees a skinny girl,
Ginger hair and imperfect teeth.
The girl is scrolling through social media
Looking at the "beautiful" girls.
She thinks sad thoughts, her stomach in knots
With tears.
Another girl is plus sized
With brunette hair in a messy bun.
Like a snake, she tries constriction.
Her rounded stomach is the victim.
She wishes she, too, were blonde.
Then, in her sad thoughts and stomach knots
She contemplates her life.
Aphrodite soon sees another.
A boy this time.
He wears a skirt of pink
With mascara, blush, and foundation.
But for others, he is a distraction.
Harsh pounding of discrimination.

"Boys can't wear makeup and dresses."

He'd echo the words, alone,
Of saddened thoughts and stomach knots
In a midst of self discovery.
He is rejected by those online.
Each comment saying to kill himself
For trying to make himself shine.

They can't see Aphrodite, but she remains present.
If she had a smartphone
She would comment on their posts,
She would show her love with likes.
She would admire their beauty.
For the ginger-haired girl, she would type

"My dear beauty, your imperfect smile
To me, makes a smile that shines
Brighter than the sun.
Your unique hair
Reminds me of paintings of myself,
Red hair blowing in the ocean breeze.
We are beautiful red-heads!"

The girl would see other comments by real people
And she would smile.
And Aphrodite would smile.

To the plus-sized girl
Aphrodite would write

"Dearest darling, I admire you.
You question your weight,
But I think it grants more of you to love!
Your hair is as beautiful as a dim twilight
Shining like small stars in the night.
The boys are sure to love every inch of you."

The comments would flow
The likes would increase.
Quickly, the girl gains confidence.
She would become conscious
Of how much she was loved.
To the boy with the makeup
It came easy to her.

"My sweet boy, you are truly gorgeous!
The world is a scene
Of grays, whites and blacks.
But with you, there is a rainbow.
Don't *ever* let anyone take that back!
Pink is your color
It brings out your eyes.
If you were to be a fruit
You would be a rare
Golden apple!"

poetry

Likewise, he would react
To seeing the comments.
He had always been too scared
To show his rainbow.
He smirked to himself
As he tossed his short hair to the side
With confidence, with pride.

With sad thoughts and stomach knots
Of suffering souls,
Aphrodite folds papers of feelings
Into shapes of origami.
Beautiful arrangements of acceptance.
No longer will she stand for self-hate
When she can see the beauty
Of loving the self.
Placing ingenuity over promiscuity.

Aphrodite sees the value in love
And the pain when it's lacking.
If someone is not loving someone else
They are getting help loving themselves.
If it comes to people fighting about rights
To love who they choose
With strength and with might,
It is Aphrodite that helps sing
When she sees the rainbow of people

She sings songs of protest, support, pride.
She must not sit to the side.

Just as she supported those in war
Today, she guides people who
Fear not what others think.
She helps those who are hurt
By the slicing daggers of social media commentary.
So when other gods or mortals
Judge her with haste
They are blind to see
The impact of her grace.

"Love is love"

She would protest
Despite color, race, or gender.
Everyone deserves love.
She'd say
No one needs to surrender.

Unmasking My Lies

Tristan McGill

Grade 10. LPS Arts & Humanities Focus Program, Lincoln, NE. Maggie Elsener, Educator. Gold Key.

I can't wear this mask anymore
It's uncomfortable, it itches.
It's starting to crack and tear.
It doesn't sit right on my face.
My face.
I used to look in the mirror
I saw the same face every single day.
It was happy, it was kind
It was mine.
As life went on, I glanced at my reflection
And changed the little things that bothered me.
Days turned into months turned into years.
The figure on the other side became a stranger
They had the same eyes, same hair,
But not my face.
It didn't belong to me.
No, not my face, but a botched mold of
What I wish I could be.
Its smile was straight and white, but cold.
Its eyes were fixed on the light, but hollow.
It had no soul.

poetry

The innocent spirit that lit up my eyes or
Formed my imperfect smile
Was but a memory from long ago.

I had to keep moving forward.
The color of the mask faded along with its features.
Its glass eyes going dark.
Its smile's stitching came undone.
Its skin cracked.
Its hair was falling out.

The pieces could be repaired, but only at a price.
The price was far too painful to bare and
I couldn't pay for it at my own expense.
My payment was the *Truth*.

I had to fix "my" face and put it back together.
It was a puzzle without outlines, nor a right configuration.
It was a problem that needed far more than glue and duct tape
More pieces fell out of place, more half-illustrated patches appeared.
I was unrecognizable not by only myself, but to the world.

poetry

After years of searching for the missing fragments, I
realized my mistake.
I was holding on to a false hope.
A hope that I would be loved,
A hope that I would be recognized,
A hope that I could be me.
That I could be me without being judged
Without being lied to
Without consequence.
Without paying the price for a product that doesn't
exist.

I take off the mask that I hid myself behind for
eight. whole. years.
The mask won't come off.
I punch it
I scream
I cried.
I cried because I was stuck burying who I had become

I bashed the mask again.
And again.
And again.
And again.

In my efforts, I had broken my spirit
And my mirror.

I took a deep breath, and let go.
The worn mask floated softly to the ground

I picked up a fragment of broken glass,
Brought it up to my face,
And stared.
And I saw a face that I hadn't seen in years.
I grew into my smile
My eyes met their own gaze.
There were tear streaks running down my face
I can finally lay my lies to rest.

I wake up and look into the mirror
It's still *my* face
I walk outside and into the city
Showing my face for the first time in years.
No one stares any more, no one notices.
I silently slip into the crowd
And just walk.

poetry

Too Cruel

Kelley Lebahn

Grade 12. Fremont High School, Fremont, NE. Kristen Strickler, Educator. Silver Key.

dramatic script

Excerpt

Lights up. It's a warm summer sunset in the 1900s. A young man and woman stand center. The man, James, holds a brand new, very old Kodak camera toward the woman, Arlea.

James

Come here, Arlea. I want a picture of you in this dress

Arlea

I wear this one all the time. It's nowhere near new. Did you just now notice it?

James

No, but I like how this one reminds me of the sky after it rains. It's very much like your eyes, like the peace after a storm.

Arlea

You're getting romantic on me again, James. Watch yourself.

James

I can't help it. I suppose it's the artist in me. Here, pose.

She poses for the picture.

Arlea

Make sure I look good, okay?

James

You always look good.

Arlea

Now you really are saying too much.

James

Ready? Three, two, one.

He takes the picture.

I don't have very much film left. I'll need to buy more. We should take a train to the city tomorrow. Hold on, I'll take another to be sure, stay still.

He takes another, to be sure.

It's going to be perfect when it prints! I think I'll keep this one in my wallet.

Arlea

Should you keep a picture of a childhood friend in your billfold? People could start to wonder.

James

Let them.

Arlea

James—

James

Tonight, my aunt is hosting a party, something small, mostly family and some of her old wealthy friends, I think. It should be incredibly dull, but I've already agreed to make myself seen. Will you come with me?

Arlea

Of course, I will. But don't you pull anything funny on me this time, you hear? Any jokes, and I'll never speak to you again.

James

Maybe that's a good incentive.

Arlea

Ha!

James

Fine, Fine, you've got a deal.

A handshake. Lights out. A four-poster bed and a vanity appears. Arlea sits as her handmaid, Rosie, fixes her hair.

Rosie

You look beautiful, Miss.

Arlea

I don't feel beautiful, Rosie.

Rosie

I know.

Arlea

I don't want to go out. The idea of dancing and promenading is making me sick. Maybe I should just stay home. I have a new book I want to read anyway.

Rosie

Yes, but you already agreed, and your father is worried you're getting unwell again. If not for your sake, go out for his.

Arlea

I am getting unwell again. It is so hard to get out of bed—to do anything, really, and I'm always so frustrated. It's like I can't go three minutes without a temper tantrum. I've been snapping at you recently, Rosie. I'm sorry for that.

Rosie

I understand, Miss Arlea. You have nothing to apologize for.

Arlea

But others don't understand. I feel like a shrew sometimes in public. And James—I think he has intentions of proposing soon.

Rosie

Miss, that's so exciting!

Arlea

No, it's not Rosie. What am I to say to him when he does? Oh, James, yes, I'll take your hand, but here's a smart surprise: I'm ill in the head, and now it's your burden to take care of that.

Rosie

I believe most girls stick with a simple yes.

TROPHY STOLEN

VICTORIA BOGATZ

Grade 8. Lewis & Clark Middle School, Bellevue, NE. Michelle Kastl, Educator. Honorable Mention.

Apple Grove Times
May 2, 2021

TROPHY STOLEN

By Ree Porter

IN APPLE GROVE, thefts are rare. Yesterday's stolen trophy was one of the first cases Ms. Teri Solver, the town sheriff, had seen in a while.

"It's crazy," Sheriff Solver told Apple Grove Times. "First trophy the town's ever won—poof, gone!"

It indeed went, poof, gone. The trophy in question was won by the Apple Grove Middle School Debate Team last month at the Regional Debate Competition. Principal N. Charge had said she was "incredibly proud of the team and their efforts."

The debate team was formed a year ago by Dee Bates and Rhodes Freeway, two Apple Grove Middle School students. It was the first club in the school's history.

"We just thought, heck, what else are we doing?" Dee Bates stated in an article by the Apple Grove Times last

humor

year. "Me and Rhodes love to debate, and we wanted to put that passion into something productive."

Ed Jucater, an English teacher at Apple Grove Middle School, sponsored the club. "I saw Dee and Rhodes' excitement and I was more than willing to sponsor," he said. "I just dragged out some podiums and printed out a list of topics, and we had a debate club. Plus I bought a gavel from Walmart, 'cause why not."

The club's size grew over the next year, and they practiced twice weekly to prepare for the Regional Debate Competition. At the competition, they won almost every debate and continued to advance, finally winning first place.

"When we won that trophy, it was amazing," Dee Bates said. "Our school even had to get a trophy case, because we'd never won anything before."

When the trophy was stolen, Bates said he cried with Rhodes Freeway. Freeway declined to comment, but Mr. Jucater said he was "looking down" after the trophy was stolen.

Principal Charge was not available for statement on the theft, but it appears a full investigation will be conducted. School secretary Iben Board confirmed this fact.

"We better get this trophy back," the school janitor, Gus Stodian, said. "It gave me such a thrill to clean that case and see the trophy that these students worked so hard to win. It's a shame."

Sheriff Teri Solver has not released any information on potential suspects, but some are pointing fingers at Strawberry Hill Middle School. Strawberry Hill is about twenty miles away from Apple Grove, and their middle school faced off against Apple Grove Middle School in the debate finals.

"I mean, Principal Charge was kind to the losing team," Rhodes Freeway said. "But Principal Powerfle [the Strawberry Hill Middle School Principal] was horrible. The entire team was kind of being sore losers. I wouldn't put something like this past them."

Ima Noyd, a student at Strawberry Hill Middle School, had a different perspective. "We started our debate club two years before Apple Grove even knew what a debate was. Except at the competition, they were acting like we were the newbies, trash-talking us and everything. They were jerks, so of course we were upset when we lost to them. But none of us was mad enough to steal their stupid trophy," she said when contacted about the trophy theft.

The mystery is ongoing. Keep reading Apple Grove Times for more information!

ANALYZING THE FRAMEWORK

The Mental Health of Students of Color

TANYA BACHU

Grade 9. Brownell Talbot School, Omaha, NE. Matt Low, Educator. Silver Key.

After months in quarantine turned into years in quarantine, and we finally stopped treating our sourdough starter like it's a new pet, baking endless amounts of banana bread and becoming BFFs with InstaCart, we finally got to watch the long-awaited 2020 Olympics. Tom Daley knitted a cardigan on the sidelines because walking around in a Speedo after diving must have been cold. A bear was roaming around an Olympic baseball stadium; who said only humans got to have fun at the Olympics? And Novak Djokovic broke two tennis rackets, which was a classic Djokovic exit.

But the Olympics was not all fun and games: the Japanese public was worried about people coming to their country, the heat levels were insane, but most importantly, there was a shift in the conversation around mental health, mainly coming from Simone Biles and Naomi Osaka. Both champions in their respective events, Biles and Osaka are notable women of color who break barriers on a national platform. People such

critical essay

as they are held to such high standards that they sometimes have to take a break and focus on themselves, but this isn't an issue that affects only high-profile athletes and celebrities. A lack of mental health awareness for people of color runs deep, and it starts where an incredibly vulnerable part of the nation needs it the most: the classroom. Mental health is neglected in students of color from a very young age, and it doesn't get better as they get older. The mental health of students of color is important to talk about because COVID-19 has made matters worse and the likelihood of racial incidents has increased drastically. Given the timeliness of this topic and the ever-increasing burdens students of color continue to bear, we must improve how we view and talk about mental health.

As a high school tennis player, a crowd of two people makes me anxious, so I can't imagine what Naomi Osaka has to go through on the national stage. First, there are two causes of discrepancies in mental health support for students of color: stigma around seeking help and no culturally competent mental health support. Initially, students of color struggle with mental health because the stigma around it silences them. What exactly is this stigma? It is the absence of seeking help and the fear of racial inequality. A survey report in 2012 by The National Alliance on Mental Illness stated that of the 765 students with mental illness the researchers surveyed, 36% said stigma was the number one obstacle to seeking help (Gruttadaro and Crudo, 2012). The benefits of disclosing do not outweigh the risks; students of color may have forced ideals that prevent them from talking about their problems and getting help. Common stigma beliefs include that those with mental health are menacing and will not get better, and that their mental illnesses are their fault. These beliefs are what lead to the negative idea that a student's mental health is unimportant and should be silenced.

Additionally, there is a lack of culturally competent mental health support in schools. There are many risk factors for mental illnesses including education, income, and environment, and these lead to racial disparities. People of color have less access to mental health services, but when they even get the care, it is much lower quality than white people's. A report by the American Psychological Association stated that in 2015, 86% of psychologists were white (Lin et al., 2018). This is less diverse than the U.S. population as a whole! Minimal diversity can leave students feeling disconnected from their counselors. Cynthia Guerrero, a brand contributor on Forbes, shared her story and said that when she brought up something about her culture, her counselor, who was white, looked at her with confusion, which led to Guerrero being emotionally drained. She never went to a counselor after this incident, even when she had mental health issues (Guerrero, 2021). When mental health counselors do not have a proper understanding of their student's culture and race, their comments and reactions can come off as outright prejudiced and discriminatory.

During the Tokyo Olympics, many people were calling Japanese people Chinese. That's ridiculous! Especially coming from people who literally cannot name even one country on a map. There are two effects from the stigma over mental health and the lack of diversity among healthcare professionals: lower academic performance and imposter syndrome. Students of color have reported steeper rates of loneliness, anxiety, depression, and hopelessness, and a huge effect is that it hinders their academic performance. Students of color are much less likely to graduate and have continuously high rates of dropouts. The pressure to engage in social justice activism and fight against racism leads to anxiety and stress in school. Students of color set aside their mental health needs to focus on fighting against racial injustice. The amount of stress they endure and the amount of time activist work takes can cause students to fall behind in their studies or become so emotionally burdensome that they drop out.

Second, feelings of imposter syndrome can start. Imposter syndrome is the feeling of self-doubt and personal incompetence that weakens you. Imposter syndrome starts in the classroom for students of color. It takes down minorities' minds and makes all their thoughts negative. It can make students not want to work hard academically or even in their personal lives. Take the story of Dena Simmons, a black college student from the Bronx. She explained in a T.E.D. Talk how her peers judged her for her accent, her roommate felt like she couldn't show Simmons her valuables, and girls judged her for applying hair grease. This led to Simmons's school life being filled with feelings of imposter syndrome (Simmons, 2017). Imposter syndrome is not easy to cope with, which is why we need to put a stop to creating stigma and increase representation in school healthcare professionals. We as a society need to address the lack of mental health support because people need to have a safe, comfortable, and understanding person to talk to.

From the 2020 Olympics, we learned that it's okay to not be okay, but how can we apply this? There are two solutions: destigmatize getting help and increase representation. There are so many little things that we all can do daily to help. We need to do community awareness campaigns: this is possible through school newspapers, information brochures, and school events. One thing that schools could do is implement curriculum-based learning programs that specifically focus on informing students about mental health issues and

critical essay

how to address the stigmatization. Teachers should address how important it is for students to be respectful and positive with their peers struggling with mental illnesses. It's important for schools and our whole community to understand that those with mental illnesses are still individuals like the rest of us.

Finally, we need to increase representation and support for counselors and psychologists in schools. Hiring staff of color for healthcare is a critical step in encouraging students to seek help; it encourages inclusivity and makes students feel comfortable and heard with someone of the same race. School officials should start specifically seeking out people of color for jobs such as counselors and physiologists. Another way for schools to hire people of color is to have a diverse team for the hiring process. If schools take these steps to increase representation, students will become more comfortable and feel safer to share their feelings.

I'm glad that the 2020 Olympics did happen after all because, without it, I wouldn't have gotten to watch my sister practice her tennis swing in front of the TV, only to have the racket fly directly into the glass. But most importantly, the talk around mental health may have stayed silent. In a world where the state of our mental health seems to be hanging by a thread, we need to follow the examples of GOATs like Naomi and Simone and raise the bar for our students.

Works Cited

Gruttadaro, Darcy, and Dana Crudo. "College Students Speak: A Survey Report on Mental Health." *National Alliance on Mental Illness,* 2012, https://www.nami.org/Support-Education/Publications-Reports/Survey-Reports/College-Students-Speak_A-Survey-Report-on-Mental-H.

Guerrero, Cynthia. "'You Know What I Mean?': Universities Need Better Representation of Counselors and Therapists of Color." *Forbes,* 2021, https://www.forbes.com/sites/civicnation/2021/08/06/you-know-what-i-mean-universities-need-better-representation-of-counselors-and-therapists-of-color/?sh=5f2220219f29.

Lin, Luona, et al. "How diverse is the psychology workforce?" *American Psychological Association,* vol. 49, no. 2, 2018, p. 19. https://www.apa.org/monitor/2018/02/datapoint.

Simmons, Dena. "How students of color confront impostor syndrome." *T.E.D.,* uploaded by TedEd, 2017, https://www.youtube.com/watch?v=8sQ2p89PoUs.

Heavy Heart, Empty Space

Olivia Achtemeier

Grade 11. Beatrice High School, Beatrice, NE. Meghan Robeson, Educator. Silver Key.

The Old Wooden Porch

I fix my gaze on the old wooden porch. Miscellaneous chairs are scattered; together they leave plenty of room for visitors. The steps that lead to the door remind me of every conversation partaken leaning over the mismatched railing. So many beautiful memories are captured in one look at the screen door, and yet a picture can't begin to pour out each recollection I hold. The plants droop and are weary in their pots, yet one stands tall: a single crimson rose. The house never belonged to me, but to another I held dear. My chest is heavy as I take one last look at the house, yet perhaps it isn't the house that I'll miss, but the person who once dwelt inside.

The Crimson Rose

I stare in awe at the garden of flowers before me. Each row appears more vibrant and lively than the next. Though they are tended to no longer, I see the loving touch that once kept them from flooding the path. I know so little of gardening, but it doesn't take knowledge to enjoy the beauty God has created. I take care not to step on the flowers reaching out from below, as if deciding their time to shine is now. Finding the small cement bench, just barely made for two, I sit down and admire the roses. How many colors could one flower hold? The tender pink gently reminds me of my earliest youth, when I could hardly even dare reach up for the petals that lie above, lest I be disciplined by the thorns below. The buoyant yellow sticks out like a sore thumb. They can't be ignored, much like the years that begin shortly after reaching the double digits. The bright, prosperous, red roses hold an air much like those after their teenage years: lively, flourishing, and ready to move up. Though the 'move up' isn't what really gives the roses their beauty, but rather, the wisdom that the elder crimson rose holds. It reveals that peace and simplicity can be greater than the desires flooding this world. Its message is powerful, yet it never boasts this truth, but rather, it submissively waits and puts the lessons that it's learned into practice.

The Sidewalk

My foot catches on the cement. I land on my knees, but slowly roll to a sitting position. Without a sound I remain on the ground and stare at the uneven sidewalk. Even as I try to leave this place, it seems to be calling me back. How could I return? It's not my own, nor was it ever. A breeze forcefully brushes over me. Aside from the air it brings, it floods me with memories. It had been a cool autumn day. Hand in hand, we had walked this path, though it was only a square block—*one* square block—it was all we could handle between my tiny, youthful legs and the other's frail, weakening muscles. A smile graces my lips, but a warm sting falls from above it. I promptly furrow my eyebrows. Am I crying? I see the other's figure walk steadily, yet shakily, in front of me. It was here that the other fell; it was here that I stood, so small and so innocent, wondering why it was so difficult for the other to stand up and continue walking. The other did eventually stand, but we didn't finish our walk—our *one* square block. I grimace as another burning tear strokes my cheek. I swipe it away. I shouldn't have fallen here; it was my fault for forgetting this bump in the path; it was my fault for forgetting.

ORANGE JUICE

SAM ROGERS

Grade 8. Hastings Middle School, Hastings, NE. Stephena Gilmore, Educator. Silver Key.

Being trans is like being an orange. You grow from this little green bud on a tree. You depend on the tree for life, but as you grow from a tiny little green sprout to a big juicy orange you fall. You realize that you don't need your tree anymore. You get picked up by yourself and start doing things. Stuff might get messy, you get sliced, diced, rolled all over. But the best part is that once you're juiced, the real you sprouts. You are no longer in that peel or shell that tree has put you in. You are raw, perfect, wonderful material. Being trans is like the pulp in your orange juice. It doesn't bother you necessarily, but it's always there and it sometimes gets annoying. People might hate on your pulp, which they have no business with. You like your juice just how you like it. You can't describe yourself without mentioning the pulp. Sometimes you have bad days. It gets stuck in your teeth, you get tired of it, it has a weird texture. But it's always there, and it has to be. Or else you wouldn't be you, would you? You try to get rid of the pulp, but it's always there. Sometimes you and the pulp have a good day. It moves along perfectly with the juice and sometimes you don't even notice it's there. When you are transitioning it's like getting rid of the pulp piece by piece. There will always be remnants of your time with the pulp. You will never forget it. But once you've gone through and picked everything out, let yourself go from your mother tree to be on your own, then, and only then, you shall be on your own to make decisions and agree that your pulp, your juice, your seeds, are yours.

Trans. I think it's a rather funny word, isn't it? Sure, it stands for transitioning from one sex to the other. Trans is awesome. But it's also rather cruel. You have all of this confusion, these mix-ups. You wonder, "Why couldn't this just be normal? Why are you cruel? Why did I let go of my mother tree? Please, please, let my feelings float away." But, it stays. It stays, and stays, and stays, and stays. The reason you let go of that tree is that you became ripe. Ready to be on your own, make your own decisions. And you know that the mother tree doesn't know you all that well and that the only person that knows you more than the mother tree is yourself. The slicing and dicing and becoming juice are rather painful. Like coming out in a way. Coming out to other people in your tree family might be harder than expected. They might turn to you and say, "Get out of my sight! Where is your stem? Where in the world is your mother tree?" and others might say the opposite. And those others are the only people keeping you together in the slicing, the juicing, the squeezing of it all. It's that there are still people who love you and your colorful sour and sweet juice inside of you and that they love you even though your mother tree has no control over you anymore and that you have shed your stem and your leaves. When you have come out, there is no hiding. You become juice.

Then there comes another issue. There is pulp. Yeah, there is no strainer to pull it out of you so it stays. You agree with it for a while. Like sitting in a big raft waiting, still having some hope left that rescue will come. But you get hungry. You and the pulp start to fight and clash. The pulp becomes unsatisfying. You fight and churn with it and beat it with your pride, but it stays. Then, you sigh and turn away. But be careful. Remember that the pulp is always a part of you. If you turn away, try to become separate, you are no more than the glass of sour, stale juice. Or the dried-up peel in the garbage bin. Once you are finally at peace with your pulp, you have realized it needs to stay, it's a part of you, but it doesn't control you. There will always be the pulp within you, but it will change. You will become you. It seems so far away but so close you can see it, feel it, try to reach for it. But time is time. It moves and shifts and all you need to do is be patient, live with your pulp. Keep going, keep hoping and someday the time will come when your peel will no longer be a part of you.

Now, I must speak of the Mother Tree. There are many types. Types that accept and love, types that push away, types that don't care, and types that aren't there. My mother tree is exceptionally difficult. She has all of these wonderful branches—strong, firm—and twigs that provide many resources. When her leaves sprout they have the most magnificent shape and color. But there came a time where a root grew on her tree. She thinks she loves the root, even though the root just makes her reek, makes her branches turn flimsy and her leaves turn brown. She has no idea that the root is draining her. The Root influences her, tells her things that aren't true. Tells her that her own fruit that she bears is bad. That my pulp is not my own, that it's a delusion, that it's not there. But I know it's there. I witness it every day. It is inside me and a part of me, you cannot take it away. It's my pulp, and I need it.

Do you want your child to be depressed, sad, lonely, and longing to be himself? Do you love the root more than you love your own children? The Root broke my mother. Made her think that I was stupid, dumb, resistant and distant. Then I fell. I was tired. So tired of feeling dried up. Her love had no more effect on me. I was ready to be free. I plummeted toward the ground. I came upon my loving Father and I cried. When I am with her, my mother tree still influences my decisions.

And I try to hide my pulp. But there will come a day where the impact is no more. I remember the times where Mother was loving and held me and made me feel safe. I hate that root. I love my mother tree. I love you. Mother Tree.

Trees are quite difficult. I know someday I shall grow into a tree, but that is a long way away. Trees are adults. When I left my mother tree I had to turn to someone. Someone to guide me and my sister through our pain. My sister and I found our Father Tree. Our father tree is great. Tall and strong. Reaches for the sun and gives nutrients to the air, and sucks water from the ground to feed our family. He has a wife, another Mother Tree. Together, they bore fruit. Now, there are three oranges on their house of branches and leaves. We call the new mother tree DD. DD is a brilliant and magnificent Willow Tree. She bears lovely soft moss and is a home for a collection of knowledge. My Father is a bright redwood tree. He is able to guide me through my life. The sun is his friend, and the ground is his buddy and together, in our weird family of orange juice and branches, we flow with the air, the weather, and the sun. I will never forget Mother. But I have no intention of returning to my mother's branches. I'm not going back for the pain of my shell awaiting me. I will stay with my strong family in the cool air and my mother will have to stick with her root.

The journey is rough for me. I know there will be plenty of good times and many bumps in the road. But I have my family to guide me and my mistakes to learn from. I have friends and parents to help me. I have a sister who is always there for me. Everyone in my life will help my seeds sprout. But, until then, I will flow in my glass, live in harmony with my pulp, live a beautiful life in the home of my father and DD. I am Sam, and I'm also trans. I have my pulp and problems. I have my family and friends. I have my community and strangers. I have the sun and ground. My regrets still haunt me but the light in my life shines through them. I am one with my pulp. My name is Sam, and I am Transgender.

Synesthesia

Clarissa Tan

Grade 12. East High School, Lincoln, NE. Ellen Jaecks-James, Educator. Gold Key.

I am seven.

I see nothing but pitch black.

I hear the audience shuffling beside me, the low murmurs of conversation accompanied by the flapping sound of concert programs.

I feel the itchy gauze covering my eyes, the *paracetamol* medication numbing my pain.

Somewhere in the distance, through the sheer curtain of gauze and my closed eyelids, a bright white spotlight appears. Around me, the audience hushes into silence.

As the cello strikes its first chord in the key of E minor, the blurry nothingness I see has been replaced by a dark stormy mass of blue. In the present, I hear the addition of hushed strings, muted brass, and low quivering bass. In my mind's eye, the mass of blue shifts to incorporate new shades of navy, indigo, cerulean, and white, mixing together then separating in waves.

It feels stronger than a daydream but weaker than my physical eyes. It's like I'm in a room, only the room has no walls and no corners, and nothing surrounds me but a pool of color. The color extends outward, into a seemingly endless space, reaching into the depths of my mind. Color. And music.

The cello's low sweeping melody seeps its way into my imaginary room, broken only by the twinkling flute, which shines its silver light amidst the oppressive darkness. In minor keys my spirit is low, but when the sound shifts to major, I'm overtaken by peace and euphoria. With brilliant touches from the flute, the room in my mind is bathed with a warm golden glow, scattered tranquility among the swirling blues and greys. Yet as the cheerful sound fades away, everything shifts to darkness again.

Agitated blobs of silver grey and midnight blue dance around each other, billowing up and down as if carried by a wind. As the orchestral dynamics grow dramatically from piano to forte, so does my world. The colors swell around me, growing in waves until every part of my imagination is painted blue. The cellist's scale ascends with it, getting higher and higher until with one final note, my colossal wave of color comes crashing down. Around me explodes a dramatic E minor chord, spraying shades of navy, indigo, cerulean, silver, and white everywhere. Empty, echoing.

As the piece comes to an end, I'm brought back to the present.

I hear the tremendous applause from the audience.

I feel the itchy gauze covering my eyes.

Yet with no music left to reach my ears, I see nothing more than pitch black.

Synesthesia.

◇◇◇◇◇

I am fourteen.

I am blinded by the bright white spotlight smacking me in the face.

I hear the audience shuffling somewhere in front of me, the low murmurs of conversation accompanied by the flapping sound of concert programs.

I feel the nervous beads of sweat trickling down my forehead, the heat burning up my neck, and my anxiously pounding heart throwing itself against my ribcage.

Nonetheless, I tell myself I'm ready.

Raising the piece of wood in my hands to my shoulder, my fully-rosined bow touches the violin strings, and I draw my first chord. Light, brilliant, cheerful. The auditorium fills with A Major, echoing sound through high ceilings and wooden floors.

The sweeping orchestral melody paints across my mind, in red, gold, lilac, rose, white, and more. As my fingers fly up the string, I dance through the endless field of warm-toned colors. The color grows in splashes with every note I play, filling the auditorium.

It feels stronger than a daydream but weaker than my physical eyes. It's like I'm in a room, only the room has no walls and no corners, and nothing surrounds me but a pool of color. The color extends outward, into a seemingly endless space, reaching into the depths of my mind. Color. And music.

My violin's brilliant harmonics add flashes of gold as my painter's reverie continues to bloom. Vibrant shades of red and pink swirl around each other in a joyful dance, enveloping me in euphoria and soaring above heavenly clouds. The higher my notes, the brighter the shades of gold, illuminating everything with a warm glow. I rise until I can rise no more, and with one final note of the ascending scale, my bow flies up into the air. *Finis!*

Thunderous applause from the audience.

A thousand springs creak as they rise from their chairs.

Triumph and exhilaration course through my veins.

I no longer play, but the music still rings in my ears.

And I see red.

I see gold.

I see lilac, rose, white, and more.

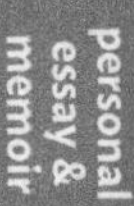

Walk to Morning Market

Clarissa Tan

Grade 12. East High School, Lincoln, NE. Ellen Jaecks-James, Educator. Gold Key.

"*Ou Teng-Xiang*," whispers my grandmother in Mandarin, "it's time for us to go."

Without opening my eyes, I grunt in acknowledgment, and roll over in bed. *I'm tired.* Three floors below us, the neighbor's rooster crows, signaling 5 AM.

In the weak light of dawn, we slowly walk the streets of Hunan, China, one cobblestone at a time. As the other aunties pass by, they call excitedly, "*Yang Shu-Han! Ou Teng-Xiang!*" My grandmother can't see them, but she smiles upon hearing their voices, and greets them in return. Unable to convert the English in my head to Mandarin, I say nothing, resorting to a wave and a head nod. As our long walk to market continues, my stomach grumbles fervently. I'm starving; I haven't had breakfast. Grandma must be hungry too, but she doesn't complain, so I say nothing.

The sky lightens considerably, and I figure it's almost 6 AM. Around us, the city of Hunan comes to life, filled with honking taxis, high-speed bullet trains, and the hustle-and-bustle of millions. Ahead, food carts are lined up and down both sides of the street, each vendor trying to out-shout the others. Here is a city within a city, where there is everything: sugary mountain hawthorn, freshly skinned meat, scallion pancakes, ripe apricots, and sweet custard buns.

I ask my grandmother, "What would you like?" Smiling, she replies, "Whatever you want."

Together, we approach the first vendor, who is selling my favorite scallion pancakes. I point to the largest size, and say "two, please." Grandma hands me her purse, but noticing the small wad of bills inside, my stomach churns in guilt. Knowing she can't see my next action, I silently pull out my birthday money: 32 Yuan (5 dollars). We continue up the market street, picking out delicious snacks and not-so-delicious vegetables, which she insists I eat. By the end, so many grocery bags hang from my elbows that their straps dig red marks into my skin. It stings; they're heavy. But I know that if I don't carry them, grandma would have to, so I say nothing.

Upon returning to the apartment, my legs are sore, my forearms burn, and my back aches. I feel like a teenager in the body of a 70-year-old. Every single day for the past year, through wind, snow, rain, and shine, grandma and I have made the morning trip to market.

I'd rather take the bus, which goes to market in just minutes without blistering our feet. I want to return to my parents in America, where we drive our own car to

Hy-Vee, where every day is not a test of my Mandarin skills, where I'm free of adultlike responsibility.

But every day, I think about the numerous sacrifices my grandmother makes for me. Despite Hunan's steel factory accident that turned her blind years ago, she continues to work. At a time when my parents are preoccupied with their jobs, sending me six thousand miles from home in Nebraska, my grandmother makes my home in Heshun.

She teaches me Chinese calligraphy every Monday, guiding my hands with hers as we find comfort in brush strokes. Knowing my love for music, she takes me to the local piano shop every weekend, and waits for hours as I play their keyboards and grands. At night, we sit outside on the porch under Hunan's factory-polluted sky, folding hundreds of small origami stars to mimic Nebraska's real ones.

As the year passes, it's finally time to return home to America. And yet, when I think about everything my grandmother has done to make Hunan my second home, despite not being able to afford much, I'm forever grateful. In return, walking was a small thing to do.

Tattoos

Chloe Waters

Grade 10. Sterling High School, Sterling, NE. Evi Wusk, Educator. Gold Key.

The first time my mother left I was five years old. It's tattooed in my brain forever. I was so confused because all I could see was the mother who I loved so much walking out the door without a proper goodbye. Nevertheless, she couldn't even send a birthday card splattered with sparkly colors. She left and I thought she would never come back. Two years later I found that I was wrong. I was coming home from my best friend's birthday party. I was so excited to come home and tell my dad all about the roller rink. I walked in through the door, trying to escape the autumn's chilling breeze, and the first thing I saw was my little sister, Christina, nestled up right next to my mother. I stood in shock not knowing what to say or do. I still remember the background sound of the TV commercials and the burning smell of the cinnamon apple candle on the coffee table. Finally, I urged myself to move.

I jumped in her arms and started to cry. I couldn't believe that after two years I could feel the soft palms of her hands on my back as she hugged me. In that moment the whole world around me was merely a simulation and nothing else mattered. I was finally the girl that didn't have to make a mother's day gift for my dad or my grandma. I was always a pretty mature kid so I knew that some things don't last forever, but at the time I couldn't help it and thought that this just might. The next day I felt like I was walking on air and nothing could bring me back to the ground. I was at recess and ran to my second-grade teacher to tell her the news. "Mrs. Niles! Mrs. Niles! You'll never guess what happened last night!" I exclaimed. "What would that be?" she responded. "My mom came back!" I couldn't even believe that those words were falling out of my mouth. Soon they would shoot right back with the same force as a pistol.

A few weeks later, my mother was sitting outside on the phone with her mom, my Nina, when I overheard her talking about how she should've never come back and how she couldn't stand it here. Every word just felt like being cut with a thousand tiny paper cuts. Just the other day I couldn't believe she was standing in front of me and now she's packing her bags again? I looked at my mom with so much hurt, with so much need that I thought I'd never stop staring. And then she was gone. This was the second time my mother left me.

I'm not angry anymore and I'm not sad. This was my life experience that I don't wish upon anyone, and I know it's not my fault. Someday I'll leave too. I'll go off to college and say goodbye to this little town. I don't have to know where I'm going or what I'm going to do when I get there, as long as I know that I have loving arms to come home to. As people come and go through our lives the ones who leave and make an impact are the ones we'll remember forever.

My memories go way back to when my big family was still intact and lessened to just a few. I grew up in a pretty big household of 3 sisters, one brother, at least 2 dogs, and my dad. It has never been the same as it was when I was little. Mariha, my oldest sister, went to college; Marissa, her twin, went into the Marines; and Tyler, my favorite brother, is now a big shot model in L.A.. So that just leaves the two last standing, Christina and I. Yes a lot of us have left but it's not as bad after a while.

I mean there's no better feeling than the adrenaline rush on the long path to Omaha's Airport to come and see my siblings again after this long time of being away. Everything that all leads up to the moment I jump into Marissa's arms and take in the cheap, tangy perfume after months had gone by without communication. The moment when I see my brother's tall, lanky body walking down the never-ending hall of the airport. These memories will forever be engraved in my mind again like tattoos. I might not have had that motherly figure, but these are my prime examples of people who inspire me to do more every day. I know they'd never leave no matter what situation it was.

The biggest of my obstacles are the toughest ones to overcome, and I am so proud of the person I am because of it. I've never had to rely on anyone else but myself. I am the only person who can get me up in the morning and go to school. We can't keep making excuses for ourselves, and this could go out to many of us. These tattoos will forever be with us and can never be washed away. We are the ones that choose which tattoos we get next and which ones we want to show, good or bad.

Weightlifting

Strengthening the Mind and Body

Benjamin VanDiest

Grade 10. Doniphan-Trumbull High School, Doniphan, NE. Andrea Turner, Educator. Silver Key.

Strength training goes beyond your muscles.

Some of the best athletes, like Tom Brady and LeBron James, take care of their bodies. One way they do that is by weight training. Forty-four states in the United States mandate that high school students earn some PE and/or weights credit to graduate, which benefits kids because it helps them build strength.

Weight training goes beyond just your muscles. It not only helps to jumpstart your muscles, but it also gets the blood flowing to your organ systems. Core weight training exercises include back squat, bench press, hang clean, and overhead press.

According to mayoclinic.org, weight training improves muscle mass by building muscle strength and improving sleep, posture, and quality of life. Weight training can also sharpen your thinking skills. Doniphan-Trumbull students have many options to take a weights class throughout the day. The student body can take a morning weights class at 7 AM or take it sometime during the day with PE and Weights teacher Mr. Quinten Hite.

"Weightlifting has many benefits. Along with increases in strength, speed and flexibility, it provides an increase in confidence and helps students build positive relationships with one another. Using success and failure through weight lifting provides student-athletes with immediate feedback on how close they are to reaching their goal," said morning weights sponsor Mr. Jordan Conner.

Weight training does not just benefit athletes. Everyone can gain from weight training. It improves your overall mobility, improves life expectancy, improves your health, and builds muscle mass. However, some critics of weight training will point out that it is not appropriate for young teens to lift weights excessively. They feel that weight training is hard on growing bodies, and young teens are prone to injuries. This may be true if the teen is unsupervised and uses improper form or lifts weights that are too heavy. However, according to mayoclinic.org, when lifting weights, lifters should use their full range of motion. Mayo Clinic encourages weightlifting for teens if done properly because it protects them from sports injuries, increases muscle mass, strengthens bones, and helps them perform better in other sports. They also feel the benefits of weightlifting, helping youth have healthy cholesterol and blood pressure levels, maintain a healthy weight, improve self-esteem, and develop proper techniques they can use as they get older.

Nicole Thompson, a Doctor of Physical Therapy at Live Well Physical Therapy, specializes in strength training. When asked about the importance of weight training she stated, "Strength training is imperative across the lifespan to promote independence, health, and quality of life. Our muscles work to support our joints, which means they have a vital role in joint health, especially at a young age. Research has shown that improved strength leads to less injury, less pain, less disability, and an overall reduction in mortality. To say it another way, strong people are harder to kill!"

Whether you are a star quarterback on the football team or a 70-year-old woman with osteoporosis, strength training can be a vital practice to enhance your daily life.

www.ingramcontent.com/pod-product-compliance
Lightning Source LLC
Chambersburg PA
CBHW010540170726
48285CB00008B/2697

* 9 7 8 1 9 4 2 8 8 5 8 6 3 *